# Smart Skills: Persuasion

# Smart Skills: Persuasion

## Patrick Forsyth

Legend 🕮 Business

Independent Book Publisher

Legend Business Ltd, 107-111 Fleet Street, London, EC4A 2AB
info@legend-paperbooks.co.uk | www.legendpress.co.uk

Print ISBN 978-1-78719-794-7
Ebook ISBN 978-1-78719-793-0
Set in Times. Printing managed by Jellyfish Solutions Ltd.
Cover design by Linnet Mattey | www.linnetmattey.com

# CONTENTS

# CONTENTS

# Foreword

Myriads of management handbooks in print purport to provide guidance on the key skills to success and business training manuals also abound. Generally, they suffer from one or both of two defects.

Sometimes, the scope of the book is too broad. Attempting to provide comprehensive advice on all the basic business activities, there is no clear message. Nobody can gain proficiency in every field of marketing and sales, administration, purchasing, bookkeeping and financial management in a short period of time, although those who start their own businesses do need to acquire a working knowledge of most. Other titles fail to distinguish between technical capability and personal skills.

However, there are a handful of personal and interpersonal skills that are essential ingredients for success in any business: the private or public sectors and the professions; large or small organisations; employees, business owners or management consultants. These are the subject matter of the Smart Skills series on which all readers can focus to advantage because mastery of them will surely enhance both job satisfaction and their careers.

The ability to persuade others is fundamental to achieving the outcomes that you want or are, at least, are acceptable to you.Whether in meetings, negotiations, making presentations, or on less formal occasions working with others skill in persuasion is an invaluable attribute. In this step-by-step guide, Patrick Forsyth explores the various aspects of persuasion and the alternative approaches you can adopt to be successful employing practical psychology in a variety of situations. As readers would expect, this further title in the *Smart Skills Series* represents Patrick at his most persuasive.

In the *Smart Skills Series* Patrick and his fellow authors bring together their know-how of core skills into a single compact series. Whatever your level of experience and the rung of your career ladder that you have reached, this book will help you to audit your personal effectiveness and raise your game when interacting with others.

**Jonathan Reuvid**

# PREFACE

'I wish people who have trouble communicating
would just shut up.'
*Tom Lehrer*

This is a good book. Read it.

If only persuasion was that easy, but it involves more than just telling. Some people seem to have the knack as it were. As the banker and author Herbert Prochnow said of sales people: "The best we ever heard of was the one who sold two milking machines to a farmer who only had one cow. Then this salesman helped finance the deal by taking the cow as a down payment on the two milking machines."

Sometimes being persuasive is very simple. The café owner saying, "Another coffee?" is selling. More often it is more complex and, whatever inherent feeling someone has for persuasion, most must work at it – many things must be got right or, however pleasantly a conversation may progress, it will not be possible to "close" (closing – securing agreement – is just one specific technique that must be acquired) and you will fail in your intentions. But it can be done. You may not always get agreement, but you can increase the likelihood of things going as you wish by going about it the right way.

Persuasive communications is a main role for some people; it may be referred to as selling and the recipients are normally clients or customers; whatever terminology is used. For most people working in organisations of any sort, and who are not or do not see themselves as sales people, persuasion is still important. You may need to be persuasive with colleagues, staff or your boss, or people more senior than you, with people who are potential collaborators, and many more

– from someone on a committee you sit on to someone external like a supplier.

Whoever you must persuade and whatever you must persuade them to do, you must go about it in the right way if you are to have a chance of being successful. This book sets out practical, proven approaches to making your persuasive communication successful. It presents powerful methods, concepts and techniques designed to win agreement and prompt action from other people.

Overall, it sets out to:

- Demonstrate the nature of communicating persuasively and show how it can be approached successfully and how any difficulties can be overcome.
- Review the techniques of persuasive communication and focus on key aspects of the process in which the right approach makes being successful more likely.
- Highlight techniques to differentiate you from other people and allow you to create a powerful case.

The ideas are presented in an accessible way and will link easily to many everyday situations in the workplace. If getting your own way is to be possible – or at least made more likely – then you need to gain agreement from other people and doing so is not about blackmail or brute force. We all want people to go along with our ideas willingly and this is not so easy to achieve.

If I tried to persuade you to cut off one of your fingers, no form of argument is likely to persuade you to do so. Yet if you have read this far then it may well mean that something persuaded you to buy this book. Persuasion may not be easy, but often it *is* possible.

The techniques that make it possible to get agreement are not themselves complicated. By and large they are pretty much common sense (or how else could I write about them!). The complexity comes in orchestrating the process in a way that deploys the various techniques appropriately, integrating them into a flowing conversation. Your final chosen approach must be acceptable to the other person and yet also present a persuasive case – one that prompts the desired agreement.

There is no magic formula and, though some overall approaches are certainly important, success is to some extent in the details.

Note: those aspects of the techniques discussed that have a disproportionately positive effect on the likelihood of success are highlighted as we proceed.

## A firm foundation

Overall, the key to being persuasive is to see what needs to be done in the right light. Whatever *you* may want, the focus must be on the other person and what will persuade *them*. Whoever they are – staff, colleague or boss – if you make a good case, then they will perceive the advantages of agreeing with you as outweighing reasons for not doing so. You have to make a case to them in their terms. You must put matters over to them clearly and in a logical manner: the logic describing what may be the many and various advantages of them taking a particular action; while at the same time you must address and minimise anything they may see as a snag.

It is not a process to be underestimated. It needs care and preparation, and often there may be a great deal hanging on what happens: you want the Board to fund a project, agree that your section needs more staff – or that you should be promoted!

## Language that persuades

One thing that must pervade every aspect of a persuasive conversation is appropriate language. Simply saying what you want is not enough. When I wrote above: *read it*, then you might well reject the thought out of hand – *shan't*. But if I say that reading this book might just help you get your next proposition accepted rather than rejected, then you are more likely to begin to take interest because that sounds like it might help *you*. This illustrates the first principle. To be persuasive you must offer people *reasons* to agree or act that reflect *their* point of view, not just say why *you* think they should do something. Such an approach demands empathy and must allow people to identify with it and with you. It also needs a systematic approach, one that is given some thought before you open your mouth and that proceeds through, building a case in a logical fashion.

To do this you first need to understand what you are trying to do; that may seem obvious – get someone to agree – but understanding how that can happen and what therefore you need to achieve along the way is important. We will start by answering the question – just what is persuasion?

# Chapter 1

# THE CORE OF PERSUASION
## Communicating to help people make decisions

'The ability to express an idea is almost
as important as the idea itself.'
*Bernard Buruch*

Clear, well-considered communication provides a sound foundation for
anyone wanting to be persuasive. It avoids misunderstandings and
others may well appreciate the clarity of it; it can enhance the profile of
the communicator in a way that impresses and can certainly act to
increase the likelihood of ultimate success in getting agreement.
Conversely, it is all too easy for something poorly communicated to be
"marked down": badly presented = bad idea. That said, let me be more
dogmatic about this: persuasion is a specialist form of communication.
It presents its own challenges and will be seriously handicapped or
jeopodised by any failings in basic communications. The importance of
achieving understanding is returned to later; here bear in mind that this
underpins any more specific techniques.

There is a danger that persuasion is undertaken without sufficient
care. It can seem easy: after all, if you know what you are suggesting,
and believe (know?) it is good, surely all you have to do is tell people
about it? Not so, as we will see. For example, a department head, intent
on conducting an orderly and effective meeting, might want to sell
people on sticking strictly to a published agenda. Sensible enough

surely, but a brief request simply to do so may still prompt argument. Why? Because with no reasons given people may draw the wrong conclusions: *it will curtail what I have to say, it will stop us dealing with X*. They may react in a hundred and one different ways – all of which fail to easily agree to do what is wanted. Matters may work out to be worse still if the manager was condescending, or in any way inappropriately abrupt or demanding.

This danger is a very real one too and disaster is almost guaranteed if you take the wrong view of the persuasion process. It is not to be regarded as something you "do to people". That makes the process seem inappropriately one way, when it should be a dialogue.

## A *USEFUL* DEFINITION

The best definition I know of selling is that it is *"helping people to buy"*. Similarly, in non-sales situations, persuasion is well described as *"helping people to make a decision"*.

This may seem simplistic, but it does characterise the reality of the process well. People want to go through a process of decision-making, indeed they will do just that whatever you may do. So, the core of what makes the basis for persuasive technique is a two-way process and both elements start on the other person's side of the relationship. Always, you must consider the way in which people assess something and come to a decision. Anyone buying products and services illustrates what goes on: they investigate options and weigh up the pros and cons of any given case (and often, of course, they are intentionally checking out several competing options alongside each other); just as you do when you set out to buy a new television or washing machine.

Whatever decision they are faced with, how do people make a choice? They go through a particular sequence of thinking. One way of looking at this, defined by psychologists way back, is paraphrased here.

## COMING TO AN AGREEMENT

One approach to this is to think of people moving through several stages of thinking, as if they were saying to themselves:

- *I'm the one who matters*. Whatever you want me to do, I expect you to worry about how I feel about it, respect me and consider my situation and my needs.

- *What are the merits and implications of the case you make?* Tell me what you suggest and why it makes sense (the pluses) and whether it has any snags (the minuses) so that I can weigh it up; bearing in mind that few, if any, propositions are perfect.
- *How will it work?* Here people additionally want to assess the details not so much about the proposition itself, but about the areas associated with it. For example, you might want to persuade someone to take on, or become involved with, a project. The idea of the project might appeal, but say it ends with them having to prepare a lengthy written report, they might see that as a chore and therefore as a snag; therefore, if the case is finely balanced, reject it because of that.
- *What do I do?* In other words what action – exactly – must someone take having agreed? This too forms part of the balance. If something seen in a quick flick through this book persuaded you that it might help you, you may have bought it because of that. In doing so you recognised (and accepted) that you would have to read it and that this would take a little time. The action – reading – is inherent in the proposition and, if you were not prepared to take it on, this might have changed your decision.

This thinking process underlines everything that must be done to be persuasive. People will always:

- Consider the factors that make up a case.
- Seek to categorise these as advantages or disadvantages.
- Weigh up the complete case, allowing for all the pluses and minuses (something that takes varying amounts of time).
- Select a course of action (which may be simply agreeing or not, or involve the choice of one action being taken rather than another or a choice being made from several possibilities), which they conclude reflects the overall picture.

Importantly, what is going on here is not a search for perfection. Most propositions have some downsides; this may be the most useful book you ever read, but reading it does take a little time that could be used for something else, therefore potentially a downside.

Think of a set of traditional weighing scales, the type with two sides, with each side containing plus and minus points of differing weight. Your job is to assemble a positive balance, one that will swing the argument. This is a good analogy and one worth keeping in mind; in fact doing so allows it to act as a practical tool, helping you envisage what is going on during what you intend to be a persuasive exchange. Beyond that, it helps structure the process if you also have a clear idea of the sequence of thinking people involve in their weighing up process.

It is after this thinking is complete that people will feel they have sufficient evidence on which to make a decision. They have the balance in mind, and they can compare it with that of any other options (and remember, some choices are close run with one option only just coming out ahead of others). Then people can decide, feel they have made a sensible decision and that they have done so on a suitably considered basis.

This thinking process is largely universal. Depending on what is being done, it may happen very quickly and might even be almost instantaneous – the classic snap judgment. Or it may take longer, and that may sometimes indicate days or weeks (or longer) rather than minutes or hours. But it is *always* in evidence. Because of this, there is always merit in setting out your case in a way than sits comfortably alongside the way in which it will be considered. Hence: the definition that describes persuasion as *helping the decision making process*.

Thus this thinking process should not be difficult to identify with; it is what you do too – witness the purchase of a television mentioned earlier. Essentially all that is necessary when attempting to persuade is to keep this process in mind and address the individual questions involved in turn, thus:

- Demonstrating a focus on the other person early on– it helps also to aim to create some rapport and make clear how you aim to put things over (for example, in what sequence you plan to go through items).
- Make and present a balanced case – you need to stress the positive, of course, but should not pretend there are no snags, especially if manifestly there are some. You must present a clear

case, give it sufficient explanation and weight and recognise the balancing up that the recipient will undertake in their mind.

- Include working details – mention how things will work, include ancillary details, especially those that will matter to others.

Thus when you set out a case, the structure and logic of it should sensibly follow this pattern. Otherwise the danger is that you will be trying to do one thing while the person you are communicating with is doing something else; and they will surely do what *they* want.

All the steps in the process must be taken before people will willingly move on to the next one. Some decisions can be taken at once while others require a pause between each stage. The core of this process is that we weigh up the pros and cons of making a decision. We all want to be able to make an appropriately informed decision; we put different points on one side of the metaphorical balance or on the other. Nothing is perfect, so what wins is best thought of as what has the highest positive balance. Thus in competitive situations a case can be won, or lost, on the basis of just one or two small points swinging the balance one way or another.

The process of making most decisions always follows this multi-stage process. But execution of the process can be complex and reflects the circumstances of the decision making. (In selling it might reflect the nature of the customer's business; the size of their organisation; the people and functions involved; their needs; the degree of influence they have on buying decisions – and what they are buying.) As an example, an organisation considering with whom to commission a major research study is likely to go through a more complex process than that of an individual deciding where to get the office stationery. Everything persuasive is best viewed from this perspective. As has been said, it is not something that you do *to* people – it is the mirror image of the decision making process – something that is inherently two-way.

Persuasion must focus on others and what is important to them. Communications are much more successful when a person's situation is clearly identified and, conversely, less successful when such information is only implied (in effect, guessed), or is ignored. Asking the right questions is thus as important to being successfully persuasive as saying the right things is (more of this anon).

Nothing is successfully agreed unless someone *willingly* agrees. There may be some reluctance but, if people feel their arms have been twisted unreasonably, they resent it and this can affect the action they then take, and at worst they may renege on their commitment. There is a need to relate closely what is done in communicating persuasively to others' points of view; this can only be done if what you say is thought through carefully. Your approach must therefore be, in a word: planned (more of this anon too).

Obtaining agreement means you must play a part in other peoples' decision-making processes, assisting them to make decisions – the right ones – rather than pressurising them into doing something against their better judgement. You must sometimes play the role, in part, of an advisor; and being regarded as an advisor simply does not fit with a high-pressure approach (rather it helps and may be worth cultivating if possible).

If the right approach is adopted, agreement is simply more likely to be reached.

With that in mind we turn to the complete process involved in what we might call a persuasive encounter.

## THE STRUCTURE OF THE TASK

Let's put the actual task facing you here, which spans a number of stages, in perspective (before getting into more detail chapter by chapter):

- *Planning:* with someone in mind, and a conversation or meeting in prospect, some preparation is usually necessary. The most persuasive people do not just "wing it", they create an approach tailored to achieve their aims and matched to each particular person they aim to persuade. At its simplest this is no more than adhering to the old adage to *engage the brain before the mouth*.
- *Handling the conversation/meeting*: when a formal (or indeed less formal) meeting is involved, it needs approaching systematically. A meeting needs some structure and must be designed to take an amount of time acceptable to the other party. Your chosen plan is like a route map, as important to assist when it is *not* possible to follow the planned route as it is when you can. The course of a

meeting cannot be dictated, it necessarily follows the events that occur and what is said to some degree even though you will want to keep it as much as possible on *your* track.

In thinking through the best approach, it helps to consider the four logical stages of a meeting:

1.  *Opening*: the first moments, making a good first impression, if necessary identifying something about the other person and their situation and setting the scene for the way you want to describe your offering.
2.  *Presentation*: making your case and putting it across in a way that ensures that it can act persuasively. How this is done, the power and precision of your description and more are vital to success.
3.  *Handling objections*: any pitch is likely to give rise to some objections – the "buts" (which may in any case only be clarifying questions) – and this stage too must be handled smoothly to preserve a positive balance.
4.  *Gaining a commitment (or "closing" as it is called in sales jargon)*: an injunction to act does not cause people to agree, but it is often (usually?) necessary to take the initiative and *ask* for their specific agreement, thus converting the interest you have generated into action.

Some orchestration is necessary. The overall progress of the interaction must be controlled and managed, and at the same time individual techniques must be deployed as appropriate and how things are done adjusted in the light of how matters are progressing. Additional follow up activity may be necessary if things are not concluded promptly. This implies a far-reaching activity. If agreement is made, then the contact may still need maintaining. If someone hesitates, then persistent chasing needs to take place, and yet doing so needs to be made acceptable.

Beyond that, those with whom you have regular contact – as a manager does with their staff, or a member of staff does with their boss for that matter – will be influenced by the ongoing nature of the relationship. We are all more likely to cooperate with people with whom we have a good relationship and to go along with what they say.

So, the persuader needs to adopt a careful, systematic and creative approach, one demanding considerably more precision in the way it is applied than the application of the traditional "sales person's gift of the gab". As has been said, the key to it all is seeing things from the other person's point of view – the classic concept of empathy – and using that understanding to fine tune approaches and ensure both persuasiveness and an approach that is acceptable to, and appeals to, those with whom you deal.

## THE RIGHT FRAME OF MIND

The way you think about the process of persuasion is certainly the first thing that conditions how well it goes and what results you will obtain. It is your attitude that decides how you will go about the detail of the task, and that in turn will influence how others see you and whether they will be willing to cooperate with you. You are, after all, usually the only person present on your side. So, in part to illustrate the approaches that being persuasive demands, consider three key routes you can take to what you do and how you do it, all of which can influence results positively. You should:

1. **Adopt the right overall approach:**

   Let's start with a single overall point that is of considerable significance. Any persuasive task must be regarded in the right way. Every circumstance and every person is different and everyone expects to be dealt with in a way that recognises just that.

   What works best is, as a result, not any one set approach. You must deploy appropriate approaches from all the available techniques and do so person-by-person, meeting-by-meeting and day-by-day. The most persuasive people are those who recognise this fact. They seek to consciously fine-tune what they do; they never get stuck in a rut but always approach what they do intelligently and judge exactly how to proceed on each occasion in the light of all the circumstances.

   This fact alone can be crucial. Because elements involved can be repetitive (the committee Chairman may have to do similar things at every meeting), it is easy to find things starting to be

20

done on "automatic pilot" and that original and creative thinking about what is going on becomes less.

Getting agreement rarely has very much to do with good luck. You can however, to an extent, make your own luck; certainly you can and will do better if you see the process of working at it as a continuous one. This affects all the other points mentioned in this book. In other words, the person likely to be of most help to you in making your communications more effective is, ultimately, yourself.

2.   Be self-motivated: It is a cliché and every book, certainly every American book, about this sort of thing discusses the need for a positive mental attitude. No doubt this can help gain agreement, but you cannot pick positive mental attitudes off the trees or buy them 3 for 2 in the local supermarket. There are, however, certain factors that do assist self-motivation in a practical sense. The wise person uses these to boost their thinking and assist their performance. Here we consider two areas that work in this way: *confidence* and *persistence*.

*   *Confidence* is a question of belief and, while it is perhaps impossible to show how to create this within yourself, certainly in a short paragraph, there is one overriding principle that helps. That is to use those tangible factors on which confidence rests. For example, if you have done your homework – you are prepared – this boosts confidence, giving you things you can be sure of which otherwise might be imponderables. Similarly, knowing your facts well, having clear objectives and arguments and what supports them being tried, tested and ready, all boost confidence. Bear this in mind as you read through this text and see how many of the topics reviewed can help build confidence in this way.
*   *Persistence* is a topic to which we return in a number of ways in the following pages. If you do more, rather than less, if you do more than others, then you know you are that much more likely to get your own way. Rarely can everything be agreed in one quick fix; some things take time or need what is essentially a campaign before matters are tied down.

Develop the habit of reviewing everything you do, and answering one basic question: what can you do to make yourself more persuasive? Then you might be surprised how much better you feel about what you can achieve.

## 2.  Resolve to constantly fine-tune your approaches

It is said that you can have five years' experience or just one year's experience repeated five times over. This is a simple yet vital principle. Experience needs to be taken and, at best, its accumulation accelerated. You should see every communications encounter you have as an opportunity to learn something that will help you make future ones work better, operating on the principle that even the best performance can be improved.

The amount of information available from past encounters may be significant; the more you have persuasive encounters the more you can equip yourself to do better in future ones. Constantly ask questions to yourself. Why did someone say that? Why did they voice that objection? Did they misunderstand something? Did they agree? What rang bells with them? If you can develop the habit of spending a moment replaying most of your encounters in your mind after you have finished them, then you can use this analysis to gradually evolve new approaches for the future.

Fine-tune the way you work and avoid getting into a rut, repeating endlessly the same phrases as if they were a mantra equally as relevant to every person you see – what you do is more likely to remain fresh and well-directed each and every time.

---

**KEY DIFFERENTIATING FACTORS**
In this chapter let's end on one with wide implications: *Understanding and using the way people make decisions (rather than just pushing for what you want) is a sound foundation for everything that must follow.*

---

So far so good; but none of what has been said to date will work well without some preparation.

# Chapter 2

# READY, AIM, FIRE
# Preparing for success

*'Failing to plan is planning to fail'*
*Traditional saying*

Planning may seem like a chore and so let's say up front that this may involve only a couple of minutes and/or noting six words on the back of an envelope; or it could involve an hour's careful discussion with colleagues. It is not exaggerating to suggest that preparation comes close to being the magic formula I said did not exist earlier. It need not take long but the rule should be that it is *always* necessary – and it can make all the difference to the chances of success. The person who runs rings around others as it were is probably not inherently persuasive; more likely they understand how this sort of communication works – and they "do their homework".

**WHY PREPARE?**
Preparation does a number of things, it:

- Clarifies the real purpose of what you want to do.
- Provides a "route map" to guide what you will do.
- Helps you plan the "shape" of the conversation/meeting.
- Lets you decide the manner in which you will operate.
- Allows you to anticipate and be ready for other peoples' responses

(or as many of them as is possible).
- Sets up your direction for the whole communication.

## THE WAY TO PREPARE

Whatever form your preparation takes, it needs to go through four stages. These are investigated in detail here, looking at the most that may be necessary; simple situations can be approached with an abbreviated version of this thinking in mind (provided they *are* simpler). The stages are:

### 1. Setting objectives:

This may sound complicated, or smack of over-engineering, but it is only a way of clarifying your thinking. It is actually little more than being sure you can answer – clearly and precisely – the question *why* with regard to what you are to do. Many exchanges between people founder because one or both of them is not sure exactly what they are trying to do. Consider a simple example: you want your boss to increase your pay. This may sound straightforward (at least as an intention!) but, on examination, it is actually somewhat vague. Consider:

- What exactly is "pay"? (Salary, benefits, annual bonus and what else?)
- By how much do you want it increased? (An extra day's pay is an increase, so is 10% more or 50% more?)
- When do you want this to happen? (Today, in a month's time, next year?)
- Many details, these and more, remain unspecified in the base description "I want to get a pay rise".

Objectives should be SMART, to use an old acronym. Meaning they should be:

- Specific
- Measurable
- Achievable

- Realistic
- Timed.

Examining how this relates to the example of a pay rise, and the simplest description of it: *I want my boss to increase my pay*, illustrates how viewing objectives this way helps us have a really clear purpose in mind. Thus:

- Is it specific? Not very – you may need to put a number, or at least a range of numbers, to it before it qualifies as a genuine objective in this sense.
- Is it measurable? Not really – practically anything qualifies as an increase; if we put a firm figure to it – 10%, say, translated into an actual figure – then it can be measured accurately. Afterwards, you will know for sure whether you have obtained it or not.
- Is it achievable? Well, that depends on how it is actually defined. If you decide to go for say a 50% increase that might definitely not be achievable – you have to pick a figure that relates not only to what you would like, but also to what is likely to be possible.
- Is it realistic? This means not "can I get this?" (meaning is it achievable?), but asks the question "should I?" It is influenced by questions such as: How will your request be seen? Will it be viewed as being reasonable? Will it mark you down as a troublemaker, or, with less optimistic aims, as a mouse? Taking this broader view is also an important part of setting appropriate objectives.
- What timing? Timing needs to be specific in two ways: first, what do you want to achieve at a particular meeting or by the end of next week? Secondly, when do you want action to be taken? Say, aiming for next month's salary slip to reflect the increased figure?

This kind of thinking simply acts to formalise what you want to achieve. It is very difficult to decide how exactly to proceed if your intentions are vague. Remember the old saying: if you don't know where you are going, any road will do. Clearly stated intentions are *directional*: that is they link logically to conducting a well-planned, well- sequenced meeting or exchange; one that is more likely to work for you and get you your own way – although it is  important that what the other party will get from the meeting is considered. Again the focus is on them not you.

## 2.    Checking the facts:

Some degree of research may be useful at this stage. Research might just be a formal word for what may only be a little routine checking. But if you try to persuade someone you have never met of something or to deal with something complex, then research may be the best word. You may need to find out something about them: what they do, whom they work for, what and whom they know and how they may think about things. This may mean talking to other people.

In a work situation it might indicate some external research. This might mean checking company directories, a website or an annual report to explore something about any organisation for which someone works. As we will see, even a few additional facts may be very useful. And making assumptions instead of using facts can be very dangerous; linking what you say to something that is not true of the other person is unlikely to ring bells.

Returning to the salary increase example, a series of simple checks – when you last had an increase, what percentage it was, what trends are current in your industry, what national cost of living figures show and so on – may take only a few moments and yet prove disproportionately useful. A meeting might stall almost instantly on a question you are unable to answer: *What's the national figure for pay increases been in the last year?*

Think here about what information you *definitely* need to have at your fingertips and what you *might* need. Doing just a little more thinking and checking in this way may prove a great asset as communication gets underway.

## 3.    Planning the meeting:

Whatever exchange is envisaged, and it may be your contribution to a meeting, a one to one discussion across a desk or a brief conversation "on the stairs", you need to have some idea of how *ideally* you would like it to go. This means thinking about the structure. What will be best for you to say first, second and third? How will you state your case? What examples or evidence do you need? How are the points you make likely to be received? And so on.

The fact that you know that no meeting will go exactly as you plan – simply because people are unpredictable – should not negate this thinking being done. A good analogy here is that of a sailing boat. The helmsman will plot a course and the straight line to a destination is worth keeping in mind. This will not be the route taken, wind and tide will see to that, but bearing it in mind will help minimise the distance that is traveled. Similarly, your task will be to get things to go *as closely as possible* to your ideal, and to be able to cope with any divergences along the way as well as doing so in a way that keeps your case as closely as possible to the way you consider ideal.

The objectives you have set will influence your decisions here. For example, if the salary increase you want is unashamedly high, then more may need to be done to get the boss to listen and take your request seriously and more evidence may be necessary to support that case.

## 4. Backing up what you will say:

Though you intend your argument to be powerful, just stating it may not be enough to get what you want agreed. This part of the planning process is concerned with what can support your case and how it can be organised.

Think how much more difficult it is to refuse a dessert in a restaurant when there is a trolley of the actual dishes wheeled unasked to your elbow – seeing is believing. Similarly you need to think about what you might show someone: a picture, a graph, detailed figures, or an "exhibit" (as when your decision about a new brochure design is assisted by the printer producing a "rough" designed to show how it will look). The range of possibilities here is enormous. You should ask yourself what things would be useful, rather than just what happens to be available, as it may be worth some effort to create things to show.

Whatever you decide to incorporate into the making of your case, make sure it is well organised. It can be impressive to produce something right on cue, perhaps from a mass of material, and it can make a greater impression if it is introduced as being specially for the other person – *I thought this might make it easier for you to imagine.*

Another thing that may, in more complex situations, add to your case is another person – two or more of you working as a team. Selecting who it should be, and sorting out who will lead, who will do what and organising it so that you work together seamlessly needs care. Well done, two (or more) people operating effectively together can add to the positive nature of the impression given. Conversely, lack of co-ordination may give a disproportionate negative impression – of a lack of organisation or lack of care, concern or competence – and do no good at all.

## 5.   Focus on the feelings of others

Preparation may not quite be a magic formula that guarantees success, but it will certainly help. So too does the factor described next. The premise is absurdly simple. You are more likely to be persuasive if you approach the process as something that relates as much to what *other people* want and how they think, as to what you want to do yourself (hence the *helping people decide* definition set out earlier). Indeed this perspective must underlie everything you do, so the starting point is to think through how being persuaded, and perhaps going along with it too, looks from the other person's point of view.

Beyond a general appreciation of their thinking, you need to consider specifically how they feel and what they want and bear this in mind as you plan to communicate with them.

## OTHER PEOPLES' FEELINGS
Most often people recognise very quickly when they are in a situation where someone is trying to persuade them of something. Their

instinctive reaction may be to dislike the idea of it – *I'm not being made to do anything* they say to themselves. However, once they begin to appreciate what is being asked of them, their actual feelings may be positive or negative, or indeed a mixture of both. Positive reactions are clearly easier to deal with and can work for you to make achieving success easier.

Sometimes – when persuading someone to do something they will clearly find beneficial – they may start to see it as a good idea almost at once. Say to someone that you want to discuss some changes to their work portfolio that will make their life easier and put them in line for a salary increase, and they will be all ears. This does not mean that they will not be on the look out in case what is being suggested is not one hundred percent good, but essentially their thinking will tend to be positive. In this case, there may well be no difficult implications for the person doing the persuading, other than to aim to build on the goodwill that is already starting to exist.

Perhaps more often though a variety of negative feelings may arise, immediately or as you get into making your case, and then you need to be sensitive to what is happening and seek to position what you do in light of it. For instance, if the change referred to in the last paragraph is stated baldly and devoid of any context or explanation – *There must be some changes* – it will almost certainly prompt objections.

For example, people might well feel:

- **Insecure**: thinking: this sounds complicated, I am not sure I will know how to decide or what view to take.
- **Threatened**: thinking: things are being taken out of my hands, *I* should decide this, not be pushed into something by someone else.
- **Out of control**: thinking: if I make the wrong decision I may be in trouble – any decision involves taking a risk and things could backfire on me.
- **Worried**: thinking: you are suggesting changes – does that imply I was wrong or at fault before? I don't like that implication.
- **Exposed**: thinking: this discussion is getting awkward, I am being asked to reveal facts or feelings that I would rather not discuss.
- **Ignorant**: thinking: you are using your greater knowledge and/or experience to put me on the spot; I don't feel confident in arguing

the point though I am not convinced.

- **Confused**: thinking: I know I ought to understand, but you are not making things clear, or letting me get any clarification.
- **Sceptical**: thinking: you make it sound good, but then it is what *you* want; maybe the case is not as strong as it seems.
- **Misunderstood**: thinking: I don't believe the case you make takes my point of view into account – it's alright for you, but not for me.
- **Suspicious**: thinking: people with "something to sell" always exaggerate and are only interested in what they want – I am not going to be caught out by this.

Who's involved and their relationship clearly affects things here. For instance, someone may have more reservations as they recognise they are about to be persuaded by someone with more age, experience or authority than they have. But a moment's thought quickly suggests all such feelings (and you may add more) are understandable, though if they are overlooked, if you go ahead as if your message should be received with open arms when in fact such reactions exist, you will surely hit problems. If thoughts such as this *are* in peoples' minds, then they can act to cloud the issue and may make it more difficult for them to see the, perhaps genuine, sense of something you are suggesting.

It is not enough to be clear or to present what seems to you an obviously strong case – the other person must see it as something with which they can willingly go along. Thus, if you recognise that such feelings exist, then you must allow for them in the way you plan and execute what you do.

### What others want
What people want may vary enormously, of course. It will relate back to their situation, views, experience and prejudices. It may reflect deep-seated, long held views or be more topical and transient – or both. Sometimes you know in advance what people want, certainly if you work with them or know them well. On other occasions it comes out in the course of conversation, or you need to ferret it out as you go along. It can be complicated – with a number of different "wants" involved together (some of which could well be contradictory) – and it can thus need some careful thought to keep it in mind. But understanding and

responding to peoples' desires is an important part of being persuasive.

Consider a simple example: imagine you have to make a formal presentation jointly with a colleague. You want to persuade them to set aside sufficient time – in advance – to rehearse the presentation together to make sure it goes well. What might they want in this situation? Maybe to:

- **Make sure it goes well:** as you do, but maybe they are more confident of making it go well than you are.
- **Minimise time spent in preparation:** like you again no doubt, but perhaps their being busy blinds them to the need for rehearsal, which they might see as being a sledgehammer to crack a nut.
- **Leave preparation to the last minute:** maybe because other tasks have, for them, greater short-term urgency, or seem to have.
- **Outshine you on the day:** they might be more intent on scoring personal points with someone than on making sure that the overall event goes well.

Many feelings might be involved depending on the nature of the presentation, how important it is and how someone feels about it; the examples quoted are common enough, however. Such feelings, whatever they are, clearly make a difference to the likelihood of your getting agreement. Even in a simple example like this the individual viewpoints are clear: i) you both want it to go well, but take differing views of what is necessary to make this happen; ii) in general you want the same thing, but would define the amount of time that constitutes the minimum needed to prepare differently; iii) here you differ, and on iv) there are very personal wants that are, to a degree, outside of the main objective involved, that of making your individual presentations work seamlessly together and be effective.

There is a need to balance the differing viewpoints if agreement is to be forthcoming. If you are the persuader, you feel your viewpoint is right – or at least that it is the most appropriate option (there is rarely ever only one way to approach anything that can be definitively described as "right"). How do you move them towards your view? Clearly doing so involves them adjusting their intentions. You do not have to persuade them to change their views completely. For instance, they may always see it as easier to do whatever preparation is involved at the last minute, but may still agree to set a time when you want or – compromise may often be involved – somewhere between your two views.

Thinking through this sort of thing so that you have such considerations clearly in mind is always useful.

## HOW DECISIONS ARE MADE

Remember how the process of persuasion was defined in terms of *helping people*. Thus, whatever the commitment is that you are looking to secure, the process of obtaining it is best viewed as one that assists people to make a decision – and which, at the same time, encourages them to make it in favour of whatever option you are suggesting.

In a purchasing situation the choices involve competition: if you are buying a television, say, then you may find yourself having to decide whether to purchase the Toshiba, the Sony or Panasonic, or whatever (as well as decide where to buy it from and what price to pay).

In other situations choice is also involved. In the presentation example used earlier, your imagined colleague will decide between rehearsing or not, rehearsing earlier or later, doing so in a way that helps them or both of you, and so on. Doing nothing may seem, in many circumstances, an attractive option and sometimes needs as much arguing against as any other option.

It follows that, if a process of decision making is inherently involved, you should not fight against it. The intention should be to encourage and *help* it to take place. Persuasive communication is not something you *direct at other people*. It is something you *engage in with them*. The difference is crucial and anything that leads you to see it as a one-way process is likely to end up making the tasks you seek to accomplish more difficult. So far so good, but how exactly do people make decisions?

This was defined earlier and the answer can be summed up succinctly – people consider the options, consider the advantages and disadvantages of each and *weigh up* the overall way in which they compare and select what seems to be, on balance, the best course of action to take.

Realistically, it may simply not be possible to select an option with no downsides. We must all assess things and select an acceptable option, one where the pluses outweigh the minuses. The analogy suggested earlier of the weighing scales is a good one. Imagine again: on one side there is a variety of plus signs, on the other minuses. The signs are of different sizes because some elements of the argument are more important than others are – they weigh more heavily on the scales. Additionally, some signs represent tangible matters. Others are more subjective – just as, in the presentation example above, achieving the right results from undertaking it (say getting agreement to a 10% increase on a budget) is something tangible; whereas an individual's desire to increase their status within an organisation through the way they are perceived as a presenter is intangible. Intangible some points may be, but they can still be a powerful component of any case. It is these sorts of factor that must pervade your thinking as you prepare, if that preparation is to be worthwhile.

One more point completes the picture here: some decisions are more important than others and therefore may be seen to warrant more thought. Where a decision is of this sort people may actively want it to be *well considered*. They want to feel that the process of making it has been sensible and thorough (and therefore the decision is more likely to be a good one); and they may want other people (their manager, say) to feel the same. In either case, this feeling may lengthen the process of persuading them.

With this preparatory thinking done, you are ready to communicate. Before you start you should know:

- Precisely what you are aiming at (note: here it might be useful to think of a personal example of something you need to do to keep in mind as you read on).
- How you intend to go about presenting your case.
- Something about the other person – and therefore their likely reactions.
- What you will use to exemplify your case (and have such things organised and ready for use).
- What problems may occur and, broadly, how you will deal with them.

33

It may also be important to think about certain other matters. For example, how much time are you likely to have to make your case? It is no good planning a blindingly convincing case that takes twice as long as you will have. Consider too: where will you be? Will there be room for you lay all the materials you plan to use out on the table?

Note: if you have to deal with people on other than a face to face basis, remember that other techniques may be involved, for example writing (maybe a written proposal) or "on-your-feet" presentation (the subject of another book in this series, *Smart Skills: Presentations* by Frances Kay), and that this can add an additional dimension to the preparation process that also needs some thought.

What happens will always contain surprises and your planning must not act as a straightjacket, but must allow you to retain an inherent flexibility. But having all this clear in your mind will certainly help; what is more it adds another important element to the equation – and to your chances of getting your own way. What is that? It is the confidence factor, already mentioned. If you are clear in your own mind of the path ahead, and have to make less of it up as you go along, then what you do will always be easier – and will make a positive result more certain. Never forget the world is full of people failing to persuade and retreating from the process, saying to themselves, *If only I had said* ... Do your homework.

---

**KEY DIFFERENTIATING FACTOR**
Simple to state: *Always do your homework, prepare and plan carefully, but see it as the basis of what to do, not as a restricting straightjacket.*

---

# Chapter 3

# OFF TO A GOOD START
## Creating the right initial response

'Well begun is half done.'
*Proverb*

From the very first moment what you do and how you do it matters: all of it. The way you go about things will directly affect your likelihood of success. Perhaps even before you open your mouth, and certainly before you have said very much, people will make judgments based on how you communicate.

Your communication style no doubt reflects your personality. So it should, certainly there is no intention here to suggest that you forget or disguise that and adopt some contrived manner in the belief that this will make you more persuasive; it won't. More likely a forced style will seem just that and may well act to make you less effective.

Nevertheless you do need to think about how you come over. Will it help your case to be seen in any particular way? For instance to be seen as: knowledgeable, expert, caring, friendly, responsive, adaptable, secure, well organised, efficient, forward thinking, confident, interested (particularly in the other person or the topic under discussion), respectful, consistent, reliable or whatever? (And what do you *not* want to appear?) Is it important that you display an attention to detail, a respect for the other person's time or that you "look the part" in some way? Many factors might be involved and such a list could doubtless be extended.

The point is not only that there are many such factors that can be listed, but also that they are *all options*. You can *elect* to come over as, say, confident or expert (to some degree even if you are not!). You can emphasise factors that are important to the other person, indeed you need to anticipate what these will be. If they want to dot every i and cross every t, so be it; you need to become the sort of person who does just that if it will allow you to reach agreement in the end.

This is not so contrived, just an exaggerated version of what we do all the time as we communicate with different kinds of people – for example those at opposite ends of the organisational hierarchy. Again, a little thought ahead of actually communicating can allow you to pitch things in the right kind of way, so that your manner enhances the chances of getting your own way – rather than negates it.

Two interrelated factors are especially important here:

1.  Projection: this word is used to encapsulate your approach, personality, authority, clout and the whole way in which you come over.
2.  Empathy: this is the ability to see things from other peoples' point of view. More than that, it the ability to *be seen* to see things from other peoples' point of view.

These act together. Too much projection and you come over as dictatorial and aggressive. Too little empathy and you seem insensitive and uncaring. You need to deploy both, and they go well together. Sufficient empathy softens what might otherwise be seen as a too powerful approach and makes the net effect acceptable.

Creating the right feel may only necessitate a few words being changed, with an unacceptable, *I think you should do this,* being replaced by something like, *Given that you feel timing is so important, you may find it best to do this*.

At this point, well prepared and with a close eye on how the other person will consider your suggestion, and in what way they will go about coming to a decision to go along with it or not, we can turn to how to structure, put over a persuasive case and, for the moment, how to make an effective start.

The communication that follows may take various forms, but from now on let us concentrate particularly on the ubiquitous meeting. This may be formal, with two people (or more) sitting comfortably around a desk, or happen on the move (walking from the office to the pub for lunch) and sometimes it will occur in more difficult circumstances (like a discussion, on your feet, in an open office or in a factory with noisy machinery clattering in the background). Always the objective is the same: to create a considered message that acts persuasively to prompt someone to take whatever action you seek.

How can you ensure you make a good start?

## FIRST IMPRESSIONS LAST

The manner you adopt, and the preparation you have done, will both contribute to your making a good start. So too will your attitude at the beginning. You need to take charge. View it as your meeting. Make it one that you will direct. This need not imply an aggressive stance. Just as a good Chairperson may not speak first, loudest or longest, you can effectively put yourself in the driving seat without making the other person feel overpowered.

---

### KEY DIFFERENTIATING FACTORS
This one influences everything that follows, so: *take the initiative and aim to run the kind of meeting you want – and that the other person will find appropriate and will like.*

---

Your first task must be to get their attention, and to make them concentrate on the issue at hand. You will never persuade anybody of anything if they are not concentrating on, and thus appreciating, what is involved. Imagine what they are thinking – *is this going to be interesting, useful or a waste of good time?* Aim to make sure that their first reaction is as you would want it. Perhaps something like – *this seems as if it will be useful. So far so good. Let's see what they have to say.*

To create this impression it helps if you:

- Appear well organised and prepared.
- Suggest and agree an agenda that makes sense to you both.
- Make clear how long the session will (probably) last.
- Get down to business promptly.

Overall, if in the first moments you show interest in the other person and make it clear that they are important to the proceedings, this will certainly assist you. Even something as simple as a little flattery may help – *Some of your good organisation would help here, John; can you spare ten minutes to go through* ... Of course, not everyone is susceptible to this sort of thing ... hold on a moment, if you just said "That's right" to yourself, then you have shown how useful this method can be!

One thing about getting hold of the meeting is worth exploring a little more, although it is relevant primarily at the more formal end of things. This is the simple expedient of setting an agenda. Let me be more specific: of suggesting the agenda you want and which you feel will make being persuasive easiest, yet making the other person feel that the meeting is useful. First, think through how you feel something is best dealt with, have it clear in your mind (and put it in writing for the more formal meetings).

Then table it assumptively: *It may well be helpful to have an agenda in mind, not least so that we can do this in a reasonable time, perhaps I could suggest* ...In other words put it over as something the both of you will find useful. Even if it is only three items – *Let's take X first and then talk about Y and Z* – this is a powerful technique. You may, especially with a longer list, prompt counter suggestions and have to compromise a little, but simply taking the initiative means that suggestions are often agreed wholesale.

The result is that you can then take things in the order *you* want. Furthermore, once the agenda is agreed, you can introduce things progressively not as what you want but rather as what they want (or at least agreed to). Thus say: *What we agreed to take next was* ... rather than voice something that starts with the word "I".

Incidentally, it is worth noting as it goes with the agenda, the duration of a meeting is best put out in the open, even if it is an estimate. If you tell people what they are likely to be in for – *Let's take half an hour or so to...* – they like it as they can then mentally position where you are in the total process at any particular moment. If people do not know whether something might take a few minutes or all day, it is unsettling, not least to their concentration on what you are saying.

## A QUESTION OF QUESTIONS

Once under way, the next stage is to find out something about the other person's perspective on the matter before you move straight into telling them what you want. This may well build on knowledge you already have of course (especially if you know the person concerned), and in simple situations may only link to a few key facts, but in more complex situations it may take up some time and unearth a considerable amount of useful information. For example, returning to the example of a presentation rehearsal, it may be useful to know whether your colleague:

- Wants to rehearse
- Needs to do so
- Sees it being done at any particular moment
- Envisages it taking a particular amount of time

Importantly, it is likely to help too to know what they believe the presentation should achieve and how exactly it might be done, and so on. Having some knowledge of this kind of thinking, and perhaps of their presentational abilities, shows you something about the job of persuasion to be done. This may range from a major battle (they do not want to do it at all), to a near meeting of minds (you both see the need, but you are going to have to persuade them to give up a longer amount of time for it than they first envisaged).

Such finding out is achieved by asking questions – and, of course, by *listening* to the answers. Each is worth a comment.

### Questioning techniques

What to ask and how to phrase questions may need some thought as you prepare. You need to phrase questions clearly and it is useful to use three levels of questioning:

1. **Closed questions**: these prompt rapid "Yes" or "No" answers, and are useful as a starting point or to gain rapid confirmation of something.
2. **Open questions:** these *cannot* be answered "Yes" or "No" and typically begin with the words what, why, where, when, who and how, and phrases like "Tell me about ...". They get people talking, they involve them and they can allow a positive feeling to the conversation.
3. **Probing questions:** these are simply a series of linked questions to pursue a point – "Tell me *more* about ...", particularly to get to the why of the matter.

The principle may help with any situation, however. To extend the presentation example: ask your colleague if there should be a rehearsal and the yes or no answer tells you little. Follow up a yes answer by asking why they think it is necessary (an open question) and you will learn more – *I'm really a bit nervous about the whole thing* – and more questions can then fill in the detail.

This kind of questioning not only produces information, but can also be used creatively to spot opportunities. Accurately pin pointing someone's real needs and formulating a precise response to them is an invaluable way to differentiate yourself. Most people not only like talking about their own situation but react favourably to this approach. They may well see the genuine identification of their problems and the offer of solutions to them as distinctly different to any competitive approach they have received, which simply catalogues what a persuader wants.

As questions are asked it is important here that people appreciate what is happening. Clever questioning may provide *you* with a useful picture, but this needs to be seen to be the case by the other party. You will persuade more certainly if the other person *knows* that you understand their position.

### More information
Two further points are worth noting here, both linked to the comment above that people need to know that you understand. You can usefully:

• **Agree the information:** using a phraseology that makes it clear that you understand is more powerful, and affects the later conversation more, than just a simple acknowledgement such as *Right*. So say something about a point, *You mention the importance of timing, this is certainly something we must consider, do you ...* linking it into further questions if necessary and making the point that you have taken it on board. You can use this later as you lead into a topic saying something like, *Earlier you said that timing was important, one of the factors here is ...* This makes what you have to say on the matter more like a response to them, than a point you wish to push. The psychology here is important.

- **Check the priority:** often people make undifferentiated statements. For example: *I suppose I'm looking for something interesting, worthwhile, but which does not take up too much time.* This is something that might be said by someone considering serving on a committee. All true no doubt, but what is most important? For example, the need to do something interesting and worthwhile might outweigh the time consideration. In other words a stated maximum time involvement might be breached if other things particularly appealed. Just asking – *you mention several things, what actually is most important?* – can give you additional and useful information.

## LISTEN TO WHAT PEOPLE SAY

It is very easy to fail to listen as carefully as you should. Imagine someone says to you "As you're not busy today ..." You disagree. Certainly you're busy. What is your mind doing? Not listening carefully to what comes next, but planning a riposte, a denial. Watch for others doing this to you; it is a classic cause of misunderstandings. There are all sorts of reasons why listeners might drift off – if you are aware how easy it is for it to happen it is the first step to preventing it.

The moral is to listen carefully, especially to the answers to your own questions. If your ongoing proposal manifestly fails to take account of them, all credibility is lost. You will look at least careless, and at worst incompetent or rude. Not good for the image.

Listening is actually easier said than done – there may be many distractions and your mind is necessarily on a number of things at once:

what to say next, what to ask and so on. There is an old saying that mankind was made with two ears and one mouth and that that is the right proportion in which to use them. So you must listen carefully and that means what is called *active* listening, a concept spelt out in the following checklist:

## Active listening to obtain information

- **Want to listen:** This is easy once you realise how much doing so can help in being persuasive.
- **Look like a good listener:** If they can see they have your attention, other people will be more forthcoming.
- **Understand:** It is not just the words but what lies behind them that you must note.
- **React:** Let them see you have heard, understood and are interested. Nods, small comments and so on will encourage the flow of information and response you are getting.
- **Stop talking:** Other than small comments, you cannot listen and talk simultaneously. Do not interrupt.
- **Use empathy:** Put yourself in the other person's shoes and make sure you really appreciate their point of view.
- **Check:** If necessary, ask questions to clarify matters as the conversation proceeds. An understanding based, even partly, on guesses is dangerous. But ask diplomatically: do not say, *You did not explain that very well*.
- **Remain unemotional:** Too much thinking ahead – *However will l cope with that objection?* – can distract.
- **Concentrate:** Allow nothing to distract you.
- **Look at people:** Nothing is read more rapidly as disinterest, nervousness and more than an inadequate focus of attention and not being prepared to engage someone in eye contact.
- **Note particularly the key points:** Edit in your mind what you are told to make what you need to retain manageable.
- **Avoid personalities:** It is the ideas and information that matters, not what you think of the person; this can distract.
- **Do not lose yourself in subsequent argument:** Some thinking ahead may be necessary (you can actually listen faster than people

can talk, so this is possible); indulge in too much thinking rather than listening and you risk suddenly finding that you have missed something.

- **Avoid negatives:** To begin with at least, signs of disagreement, even visual one, can make people clam up.
- **Make notes:** Do not trust your memory. If it is polite to do so, and the matter has sufficient complexity, ask permission and do it.

Note: this checklist is adapted from that another book I've written for this series: *Smart Skills: Meetings*.

All of the above will help you listen more and miss less; and both can make a difference.

Make no mistake. Finding out can give you information that becomes the basis of successful persuasion. If your fellow presenter lets slip that their boss has said this "better go well", then later you might use that as part of your argument – given what your boss said about it, perhaps the time we spend beforehand could be a little longer. Any conversation can produce opportunities to do this if you really listen; as in LISTEN. Besides, people love to be listened to, so it all helps create the right feeling for the conversation.

---

### KEY DIFFERENTIATING FACTORS
Here it is: *asking questions, listening to the answers (and taking notes if necessary) and proceeding on the basis of the knowledge you then have in a way that shows you are using it, is invaluable.*

---

### AN INDIVIDUAL APPROACH
It is said that there are two kinds of people in the world: those that divide people into categories, and the rest. More seriously, everyone is an individual and must be treated as such. For example, some people want to tell you more than others, some demand great detail, every 't' must be crossed and every 'i' dotted. Some are fixed on one or more specific parts of what you are saying: the technicalities perhaps or the costs.

Showing respect for someone's individuality, taking an accurate view of how they work, and getting onto their wavelength early on in the proceedings will always help you in any encounter. Persuasive technique is not, after all, something to be applied slavishly or by rote, but something to be deployed intelligently case-by-case. And what dictates exactly how that deployment should vary is the other person. Everyone is different, and it is a dangerous mistake to treat them as if they were all alike.

Another aspect of this is the standard "spiel." If someone feels you are reciting a standard litany in no way matched to them or how they feel, they will never find it persuasive, and at worst may be switched right off by it.

**KEY DIFFERENTIATING FACTORS:**
It is worth noting this in this way too: *treat people as individuals, make your proposition not just good, but right for them.*

This first stage will not last that long, but at the end of it you should feel things are well under way – and the other person should be feeling that what you are saying is interesting and off to a good start, and want to hear more.

You should also be well on the way to establishing any authority you need and be able to move ahead on the basis of a reasonable and accurate view of how the other person is feeling and thinking.

Taking the time and trouble to make a good start, and finding out from other people how they feel about things (some of which you will know in a general sense if you deal with them regularly), is the first step towards ultimate success.

# Chapter 4

## MAKING A POWERFUL CASE
## Key tactics to guarantee persuasiveness

'The meek shall inherit the earth,
But they will never increase market share.'
*William McGowan*

Once you are into a meeting or conversation, the major job of persuasion starts in earnest. Whatever you must do to put across your case (this can include description, illustration and perhaps even demonstration) must be done carefully and in a way that increases the power of the picture you are building in peoples' minds. You must also differentiate, as it is here that people are not only weighing up what you say, they are making their most direct comparisons with any other options that they may be considering in parallel: ask your boss for funding for a project and ten to one there will be someone else with other ideas as to how that money should be spent.

It is always sensible to assume there are other options and never to assume that they are anything but compelling. The factors reviewed in this chapter are all directed at increasing the effectiveness of what you do in this central area of the persuasion process

### WHAT BEING PERSUASIVE REALLY MEANS
Remember that people want to make decisions their way. They want to

think about whatever proposition you are making to them, they want to assess it and make what they would regard as a considered decision.

An effective approach must take this thinking process (described earlier) into account and match the thinking – so that what you do really is seen as helping people to weigh things up, but it must also be persuasive, your approach must work for you as well as fit with the thinking of others.

## Language appropriate to persuasion
The overall tone of what you say, and the ways you use language as you try to persuade, are all important. As a first step to illustrate a sales orientated approach, note that you should:

- Avoid an introspective tone, if every sentence, paragraph or thought begins with the word "I" – *I will ... I can* ...and worst of all *I want*, it creates a "catalogue" approach, a list of things from your own point of view, which becomes tedious and is not likely to prompt interest in whoever it is to whom you are talking. Try rephrasing any such sentiment starting it with the word "You". It will sound very different. Thus: *I would like to point out* ...becomes something that begins *You will find* .... If the latter continues by explaining why people will find something interesting, better still.
- Avoid circumspection. A persuasive message is no place for *I think – I hope – probably – maybe* or *perhaps*. You need to be positive and have the courage of your convictions. Ideas and suggestions, or anything for which you seek agreement, must reflect your confidence in them. So phrases like *this will give you* ...are better. Similarly avoid bland description. Your idea is never just very good. A suggested feature should never be stated as being quite interesting. You need to use words that add drama and certitude.
- Make what you say flow. As with any complex message, you will need a clear beginning, middle and end, no labyrinthine explanations and a shining clarity throughout. In context, here it is often important to allow how you put something over to project something of yourself. Make sure it is not formulaic as if you had

written out the best way of expressing it and are reading it out. If you want to sound friendly, efficient, or professional, whatever, make sure such characteristics show in your voice and add to how persuasive you sound.

Beyond that, what do we really mean by "persuasive"? A dictionary definition might be: to cause (a person) to believe or do something by reasoning with them. Fine, but the question is how to do this. To be persuasive, a case must exhibit three key characteristics. To perhaps more usefully define "persuasive" as a communications approach, it should be seen as:

- Understandable
- Attractive
- Convincing

None of these on their own is enough to secure agreement, and together they must not only make a strong case, they may also need to differentiate your case from competition and do so powerfully enough to make you and what you suggest first choice. As we have seen, persuasion must be based on others' feelings and situations, and identifying these is a priority.

Using this knowledge is a priority too. There is no point in asking someone a number of questions and then manifestly not taking their situation into account as you go on to explain in detail what you want them to do.

Perhaps the first rule here is that your approach must be individually tailored to give each and every person what they want, an approach which they see respects their point of view, which matches their situation and so generates more immediate interest. Differences are quickly apparent if, for instance, you think about communication up, down and around an organisation – everyone is different.

Bearing this in mind will get you off on the right track and will quickly show why a degree of preparation added to by obtaining the answers to some well directed questions are both so important. But this is a complex stage; there are many disparate things to be done; yet the whole stage must proceed smoothly. This is important to your personal positioning: if it is handled smoothly, if it appears well thought out and relevant (because it is!) then anyone you are dealing with will conclude they are dealing with a "professional" and take more serious note of what you say.

Now, we consider in turn the three key criteria that, together, create persuasiveness and how you can put them to work:

## 1. Making what you say understandable

It is probable that more cases fail to convince because of lack of (easy) understanding than for any other more complex reason. This is certainly true if the topic under discussion is of any complexity. Let's remind ourselves of the reason: it's simply that communication is not easy. The chance of misunderstanding is ever present between two people with different backgrounds, experience, intentions, prejudices and points of view.

This may involve the different interpretation of one word – for example, just how fast is immediately? In terms of providing information, this may mean that someone will see to something when they are at their desk tomorrow morning and get the details in the post that day. But someone else might reasonably assume they will have the details by e-mail within the hour; more precision is needed to avoid this sort of confusion. And that example relates to just one word. Alternatively, it may be that a long disjointed explanation of something that needs explaining ends up confusing rather than informing.

So, the first rule is probably to be careful, not falling into the trap of thinking that communication is entirely straightforward, but making sure that you choose words carefully and make sure that you work at being clearly understood. Similarly, avoid repeating slavishly something to a list of people, all of whom may differ in their thinking sufficiently to need a different approach, one that reflects them and their situation. For example, if you are trying to recruit people to a project committee the case you make to an experienced person may need to be different from that used for someone younger, who would manifestly get useful experience from it.

Remember too that people are really impressed by good explanation: something that they expect to be complicated but which turns out to be straightforward. This is a good basis for giving a good impression, and for positioning yourself as knowledgeable and authoritative. What else helps guarantee that you achieve real understanding? I would mention four factors:

(i) **Structure:** the logic of any message is crucial. This means taking things one at a time, in bite sized pieces that both you can deal with manageably and that the other person can comprehend, and flagging or "sign posting" what is being done. Thus something that begins, *You will want to know something about what we are trying to achieve, how you can help and what sort of time commitment is involved. Let's take your time commitment first, then* ... is likely to be followed more easily than something that just jumps in and deals with points at random. If someone knows what is coming and already sees it as being a sensible approach and likely to be what they want to hear, they will be more receptive.

It also stops them taking mental digressions as they say, Where's all this going? Indeed knowing your initial thinking is clear and appropriate impresses and gives some advance credence to what is to come. The antithesis, what I call the "and another thing" approach, where what is said is apparently at random and unprepared, and much less designed to be appropriate to the individual, is much less powerful and may fail to make a case at all.

(ii) **Sequence:** this goes logically with structure. There needs to be a clear and relevant sequence to the way that you go through something, and again you should make this clear to people in advance (as was done, for instance, early on in this book).

For instance, if you are selecting a conference venue, a viewing of one will be improved if whoever is showing you round decides on a logical route. This might perhaps be one that reflects the order of the day: the reception area, the meeting room, where breaks will be held, and so on. Every meeting, every conversation, needs thinking about, and organising, in this sort of way to make sure that one, two, three does not become two, three, one.

(iii) **Visual (or sales) aids:** something visual always makes things easier to understand. An estate agent has the whole property to act as a visual aid, but very much simpler things can have the same effect. A picture is worth a thousand words the old saying has it, and there is a great deal of truth in it. A graph may make a point about cost effectiveness in a moment (think of how a pie chart does this), when it might otherwise take many minutes to explain; photographs, charts, brochures, all these will help you to get your message over. Even showing a potential committee member a copy of the minutes of the last meeting may help: not because they read them, but because they can see that they are only a couple of neatly laid out pages and that says something about the meetings. See what items are available to hand. Create more if necessary – and use them; more of this in a moment.

(iv) **Description:** Do not just tell people something, paint them a picture. Some people rarely use an adjective in describing a case, yet it is essential that people see what you mean. You must stir their imagination; perhaps saying, *This could just change your life*, rather than, *I think you will find this interesting*.

Using bland language dilutes persuasion, and dilutes the impression you want to give by default. Using it is not a very good approach – let us rephrase that: it is a disastrous approach that can kill the prospects of gaining agreement stone dead.

Any loose and inappropriate phraseology can dilute your message. A good example here links to figures: nothing is about 10.7%, it is either about 10% or you need to quote the exact figure. A phrase like about 10.7% will cast doubt on your numeracy and on every other figure you may use in your argument to bolster your case.

In presenting your case, this aspect rightly comes first; understanding is the foundation upon which the rest of the persuasion process rests.

## Beware of jargon
Nothing dilutes understanding more easily than inappropriate use of jargon. Jargon has been called "professional slang" and is particularly

used in the context of technical matters. Between people of like understanding it can act as useful shorthand. Within my own firm no one has time to say "'all comers' seminar" (meaning a training event promoted by, say, a management institute and attended by people from several different organisations), so we say "GT course". I can't remember how this started, it stands for General Training, but we all know what it means and using it saves a second or two. It is meaningless, however, to clients and no such phrase must be used externally or it will cause confusion.

What is worse, when this sort of thing does occur, you may not detect such confusion. People do not always react at once to use of jargon. They do not interrupt and ask what it means (not least because they may fear they should know and do not wish to appear stupid). They let it go by and hope the overall sense of what is being said will be clear as the conversation progresses. But if this sort of thing happens very often, they do take notice; and quite possibly their understanding is reduced, or they do get lost, have to ask and then resent the need to do so. Either way your credibility suffers.

So watch out for jargon, especially as for most people its use is a habit (if so, become a recovering jargonaholic as soon as possible). It comes in two varieties: corporate jargon and technical jargon:

- Corporate jargon is that used within any organisation – formal or informal; it often reduces things to sets of initials – these describe the products, systems, processes, people, departments, all the things to which reference is made often and where a shorthand description is therefore useful – provided everyone understands it. It does not need to be a large corporation. Small entities are just as liable to use jargon. For instance, my wife is involved with a hospital charity and if I see minutes of their meetings some of their content seems like a foreign language to me.

- The technicalities of an industry or specialist area can also give rise to jargon; some more so than others. Computers and everything associated with them are a case in point, one with which we are probably all too familiar. The machine on which I prepared this book is a marvel of modern technology. But its manual has a nightmare lack of clarity. The language in it seems to be 90% jargon and assumes that the user has a particular level of understanding that makes this appropriate, this despite the fact that it would be perfectly possible to write most of it in plain English.

This makes a good final point: the important thing with jargon is not so much to avoid all the technicalities, but to make sure – absolutely sure – that they are pitched at an appropriate level for those to whom you speak; each of them individually. In addition, some technical or quasi-technical phrases become so hackneyed that they lose all meaning, I once asked a friend in the computer world what exactly the phrase "user friendly" meant. He thought for a moment, then said: "I suppose it means it is very, very complicated, but not as complicated as next year's model!" Some descriptions just get past their sell-by date, as it were.

Once upon a time, "user friendly" might have been a neat description, but these days, when it has been repeatedly applied to every gadget in the visible universe, it fails to add any real power.

Every specialist area, however simple it seems to those in it, has its own jargon and a range of people to be dealt with at differing levels of technical competence; so an important thing here is to be on "jargon-alert" and watch out that you do not inadvertently dilute the understanding you promote by letting inappropriate jargon slip in.

To use (but also explain!) some jargon about jargon: adopt a NUJA approach (that is: Never Use Jargon Automatically). Of course it can be useful, but it may also dilute understanding and its use always needs some conscious thought.

---

**KEY DIFFERENTIATING FACTORS**

No one will ever be persuaded by something they do not understand or which is presented in a muddled way implying that the presenter is not truly clear, so: *be certain you are completely and easily understandable.*

---

## 2. Make what you say attractive

It is one thing to be understood, it is another to make your descriptions truly attractive so that people want to listen and are keen to let you complete the case you want to make. So, how do you do this?

You must talk benefits (okay, another jargon word, but I will explain).

Consider products and services: the base principle here is that customers do not buy products and services for what they are, they buy them for what the products or services do for them or mean to them – for their benefits. Many people know the phrase about selling the sizzle and not the sausages, and the head of a cosmetics company, Elizabeth Arden, is reputed to have said, rather less kindly, "I don't sell cosmetics, I sell hope." Both statements link to this principle. To take a general example, people do not buy precision drills (what they are), but the ability to make precision holes (what drills will do); and they will only want that because of some deeper need, to repair the car or put up shelves.

The benefits can range wide too. Different people may go on holiday, even to the same place, for very different reasons: for rest and relaxation, for adventure or activities, to explore new cultures and so on; and may do so for different background reasons too: to reward their hard work or impress the neighbours, perhaps.

The principle is the same for anything: your boss will not give you that salary increase because of the amount of money it represents for you; they will do it because of what it does for them – perhaps believing it will retain you in the organisation longer (assuming they want that!) or increase your productivity.

This is probably the single most important tenet of successful persuasion; yet the world over there are many people talking predominantly about features, factual things about the item or issue, when they should be talking benefits. And, as a result, there are too many cases failing to be made as people with their eyes glazing over say to themselves "So what?"

Talking benefits, and indeed leading your argument with benefits, is a key element in making what you say attractive. Doing so is not so very complicated, yet perhaps because it is counter intuitive: we want to tell people about something and it is somehow most natural to talk about features – it can take conscious effort to state things the other way round.

So, the first task is to recognise which is which, feature or benefit, and it is useful to think through what you are discussing listing benefits first and seeing how they link with features. Consider a simple product example: a particular car may have a 6 (forward) speed gearbox (a feature), telling someone this may seem just like another piece of technical information, prompting the response, mentally or verbally, "So what?" Worse an inexperienced driver may worry that it is more complicated than they can manage. But, let us say that the sales person has identified a need for economy, then he can talk first about low fuel consumption and money saved (both benefits), quoting the feature of the 6-speed gearbox as a reason that makes that possible. Often one feature may, of course, link to more than one benefit. In the case of the car, reduced engine wear and smoother, quieter high speed cruising may also result from there being a 6-speed gearbox rather than 4/5. Try thinking this through with something a little more technical in mind (ABS brakes or torque, perhaps, in the case of the car) or applying it to your own situation.

All the description you use can be handled in this way. And, as a result, you should avoid the use of phrases that mean a lot to you, but which fail to explain the full meaning to someone else. For instance: imagine you want to move house. You must sell your own property and are trying to choose which estate agent to appoint. One estate agent may claim to have wide coverage of the area. Meaning what exactly – a very large, flat office spread over an acre? No: what they would probably say, if made to extend the point, is that they have an extensive chain of offices, use all suitable newspapers to advertise locally (and maybe nationally as well), so that more people see the details, are prompted to make contact to obtain more information and arrange a viewing and that the chances of a sale, breaking the chain, and of your being able to move before the start of the next school term, are high. This is not suggested as the exact way they will say it, rather to make the point that the first short statement about wide coverage is actually only describing features. Only as it is explained – continuing the thought that begins with *which means that* – does the description turn to focus on benefits and become both inherently more interesting and more closely linked to the actual need of someone with a house to sell.

The tendency to allow short statements to do the job of a better explanation is a very common fault, one that can ensure that the power to persuade is short-changed; beware, when you have something to describe. Do not assume everyone else will interpret every word or phrase exactly as you do. This is a particular danger with certain words. What is a practical plan or a flexible approach other than insufficiently clear?

Returning to the example a moment longer, the best sequence for the estate agent to use will put the benefit first; maybe: *We will maximise the likelihood of a quick sale, and maximise the number of people who see details by …* then, as they describe how they will do that, they list the features.

Talking benefits in this way as you describe something is a vital part of the task of being persuasive. It is important to get it right; a Chairperson should not say being on the committee is "worthwhile". Doubtless it is, but the benefits to an individual who agrees to serve are more personal: it may give them a specific profile in the organisation (or more widely in the business community, with a trade body, say); allow them to meet certain (useful) people; or get certain action in train. The detail and amount to be said depends on the individual, of course, but essentially what being worthwhile means must be spelt out in terms of benefits.

Let us define another factor in play here: if you lead what you say with benefits, then features fall naturally into place as what makes benefits possible. A car might offer good fuel economy, because it has a 6-speed gearbox. Remember also that everyone is different, and in some cases you may need to be persuasive to a group of people who all have influence on a decision, as with a committee or a board of directors. In either case, people will have their own needs and agenda and benefits must be presented so that they relate to all the individual situations and points of view involved.

**Relating benefits to individuals**
The tailored nature of the approach that is often necessary has been mentioned before. Linked to talking benefits it is a vital part of what can make you persuasive. It is one thing to define what the various benefits and features are, but that does not mean you have to throw every conceivable benefit about indiscriminately at everyone in the same way. Two things are important here: suitability and comprehensiveness.

● **Suitability:** In the example of a car, fuel economy was shown as a benefit provided by the feature of a 6-speed gearbox (though, for the record, this is not the only contributor to the level of fuel use, of course). However, the usefulness of this benefit depends on the individual customer actually being interested in economy. Someone buying a high performance, prestige car such as a Ferrari might well not care how far it goes on a litre of fuel, though they could be interested in other benefits produced by the same feature – high speed cruising being quieter and more comfortable in a sixth gear. So, benefits must always be selected intelligently to match peoples' needs and priorities; this can be as simple as stressing timing issues to one person and costs to another.

- **Comprehensiveness:** Overheard: Early on in a sales meeting the potential customer asked: "Perhaps you could give me some background about your company?" – "Certainly", came the reply, following which they did not appear to draw breath for 25 minutes. The sales person described chronologically the company history, its start, development, ups and downs, the people, customers, services – ad nauseum. Each piece of information was well described, everything that was said was true, but most of it was simply not relevant to the customer, who had probably expected 25 sentences, or even words, rather than 25 minutes.

Comprehensiveness is never, or very rarely, an objective; whatever it is you are trying to be persuasive about, achieving comprehensiveness just takes far too long. Most people are busy and they expect you to concentrate on what is most important – to them. You must often have all sorts of information at your fingertips in terms of benefit, but you must then select from it, picking those benefits which you judge are most likely to make the case you want, and using those, in the right order and the right way, to achieve what you want – and do so succinctly. Do this and your proposition will seem more attractive to more people.

Note: At the same time any case must have sufficient weight in order to persuade. Just one reason, however beguiling, may fail to do the trick. Some interesting research seems to confirm this. It has been shown that five is the optimum number of benefits to make success most likely. That does not mean that four or six are wholly inappropriate, taken as a guide to what gives a case significant weight; four to six main points seems about right. To be fair the research applies in the commercial world and relates to businesses making formal presentations as part of what they do to produce business, but the point makes sense and has, I am sure, general application. (For the record, see: *Killer Presentations*, Nick Oulten, How to Books).

## Deploying different types of benefits

Another factor allows benefits to be deployed more precisely. There are three different types of benefits and each presents different opportunities to make your case appear truly attractive. Returning to the thought of seeking a pay rise as an example, these are:

- Benefits to the person (your boss) in their job: they may want to know you will stay longer or be more productive and that that will help them achieve the objectives for their team and thus be able to meet their own job objectives better.
- Benefits to the person as an individual: they may feel that their personal relationship with you will be better, and so as a result will be your work (and that you will stop wasting time dropping hints).
- Benefits to others who are important to your boss: if you work more effectively and performance increases, their boss will think well of them.

Using the full range of benefits available and relating them to all possible situations can increase the power of what you say. So too can combining this sort of statement into a logical sequence so that all the listener's needs are met.

For example, someone (an estate agent) might say: *The advertisement we recommend is 10x6 inches and includes a photograph (features). This means it is most likely to be seen and will give sufficient information to prompt enquiries (benefit).* Thus you get viewers with a real interest coming along promptly and increase your chances of a quick sale (benefit and need satisfaction). Again there are various ways to phrase this; indeed it might be more powerful still with the benefit leading: *To get viewers with a real interest coming along promptly and increase your chances of a quick sale...*

The more you work with the concept of benefits, the more adept you will become at putting things in terms with which others will most readily identify. You can turn your thinking about anything into a form that reflects this concept. As a further example consider a wedding. The bride wants the day to be memorable. This sounds easy to agree with, but someone saying that the gardens of a particular potential venue will allow wonderful photographs to be taken is more likely to persuade a proud father that it is worth paying more to gain this advantage.

Time and care spent on getting the core description of something right – focused on what it will do for the individual – is vital. Without this any description will be pedestrian and unlikely to top any alternative offerings being considered; with it you differentiate and create an immediate edge.

**KEY DIFFERENTIATING FACTORS:**
*You must understand the benefits of what you suggest and: choose and prioritise what you say carefully and lead with what things mean to or give the other person.*

### 3. Add credibility

The third element key to being persuasive is the need to make what is said convincing – credible to the listener. It is a fact that often many people have some inherent scepticism towards anyone being persuasive; why else do we say, "I wouldn't buy a second-hand car from them", and use it as an insult? People believe that the persuader is likely to have a vested interest, they believe that they need to be sceptical and, if a good point is made about something, their first reaction may be to think: "They would say that, wouldn't they?" So, understandably enough, they want proof.

The main form of evidence, certainly the one that builds in best to the benefit orientated conversation you should be conducting, is the features. Presenting benefits followed by features focuses on the other person and offers linked proof so, as touched on earlier, in a statement such as: "This model will give you the low fuel consumption you want and reduce your motoring costs, because it has a 6-speed gearbox". There is factual, physical proof here; someone can see and touch the gear lever, and is reassured that it really exists and it is not just a sales ploy. Such proof may be asked for and, even if it is not, it should be built into the argument you put across as it is an inherent requirement if you are to be persuasive. Never rely solely on your own argument, build some real proof into the case you present.

More proof may be needed than can be provided by features alone and, in particular, people may demand, or appreciate, something from some outside sources, independent of whomever they are dealing with and, if there is one, their organisation. Here you may need to do some assembling of the kind of point that can be made to offer such external proof. There are different independent authorities to be quoted in different fields. For instance, all the following are sources of independent opinion and thus provide proof:

- An award of some sort received by, say, a restaurant (or a rating, like a car magazine testing the fuel consumption of a car; there can be quite a range of things involved here).
- A link with another respected entity: between a surveyor and an insurance company, or an architect and a planning consultant perhaps.
- Sales figures may have this impact: the estate agent with the greatest number of sales in the area (or the amount a charity lunch raised quoted as you try to get a sponsor for the next event).
- Experience: twenty years involvement in something (and the time can be independently checked) may well mean something in terms of quality or reliability. Comparing a proposed project with one the other party experienced going well gets their mind focusing on the similarities.
- Positive editorial comment in the press and other media.

You can probably think of more and certainly need to think systematically about any case you plan to make so as to assemble all possible proof factors that can then be kept in mind to be selected and used when appropriate.

An additional, and sometimes more powerful, form of proof is that of testimonials or references: in other words evidence of past successful experience. A company making even general mention of the kinds of people they already deal with to a potential new buyer can add reassurance. Specific past names quoted may be more useful than just a hint of "someone". For this they may need to get permission so that they can say, for instance, Patrick Forsyth is a regular user of our services. And such people or organisations need to be selected carefully. Quoting to a small company that you do business with several large multinationals may put them off, and vice versa. Similarly if you quote a company, which is competitive with another, this may just annoy them; and if they are so dissimilar that they feel they do not compare this may add nothing to the argument. So, for the committee, different existing members might be quoted to several potential new recruits. Whatever reference of this sort is used must be quoted in the belief that it will impress – if that is the case, this must be good.

Returning to the example of the presentation again, credibility might be added in various ways:

- Quoting past experience: the project approach is very like ... and that worked well.
- Involving the support of others (a person or organisation): the Training Manager says a rehearsal would be useful (when the other party respects the person referred to).
- Quoting measurement of results: 50% of this kind of presentation end without securing agreement, let's make this one of the successful ones.
- Mentioning any guarantees, tests or standards that are met: we must not overrun and this will help ensure we keep to time.
- Invoking quantity that reinforces the case: several of our colleagues work this way (then maybe focusing on one example).

The right supporting evidence of all sorts, fielded in the right way, is powerful in adding credibility to a case and to strengthening differentiation. Have the right evidence ready, and use it wisely and, if circumstances permit, make sure it is something external and tangible. If the salesman says the car will do 50 miles per gallon, do you believe him? Or would it carry more weight if he said that independent tests (which he quotes) say that it does so? I suspect there is no contest for most of us and, if that works for us, similar things will work for those we aim to persuade.

Thus, perhaps, the Chair person should not say that being a serving member takes about four hours a month; he might better say, John's been a member for a year or so now, and he tells me he finds it takes up about four hours a month.

---

**KEY DIFFERENTIATING FACTORS**

Remember that power can come from other factors than "what you say": *assemble and add evidence to make what you say credible.*

---

Beyond these three key elements, which together can contribute so much to persuasion, there are various further techniques that are useful to ensure that putting over your case goes well.

## SO FAR SO GOOD?

During the dialogue when you are describing your case, perhaps necessarily, you will be doing most of the talking; but you should not be doing it all. You need to have some feedback as matters progress to check that you are on target. It is easy to let your enthusiasm for getting across your message make you talk uninterrupted; yet people do not value a monologue so much as a conversation in which they are involved. Indeed anything else breeds suspicion. They appreciate your checking periodically to see whether you still have their interest, whether they understand and whether what you are saying continues to be relevant to them.

Simple observation helps; some obvious signs of acceptance or rejection you will see at once provided you look for them. Nods, expressions and a person's manner will all provide clues as to what reaction you are getting. But you need more than this; your conversation has to include checks such as: "Does that make sense?" or "Should I give you more details of that?" Such questions need not be complicated, and if some of them are open questions – that is they cannot be answered with a simple yes or no – then you will obtain actual comment as to how they are feeling. Ask, for example, "How well does what I am saying tie in with the kind of approach you have in mind?"

Not only is the feedback valuable, the information provided is like having a hand on the tiller in a boat, enabling gentle changes of course as the voyage progresses and as wind and tide change along the way. The whole process improves the accuracy of what you do and the likelihood of agreement resulting from it.

## Charting your progress

Perhaps an extension of checking progress is provided by the technique of summarising. This is always useful, but the longer a discussion is, and the more complicated it may become, the greater the need is to keep it well organised. If you are directing the meeting and proceeding in a clear, structured manner then people should keep up with the argument; however, summarising briefly as you go along will help make sure everything remains clear throughout. You do not want to give the impression of extending the meeting unnecessarily, but you do need to recap occasionally, especially on topics that are important.

This can be done as a help to both parties and signposted as exactly what it is: "Let me just summarise at this point; it seems there are three main criteria that have to be met; first, ...". Or you can just make it a part of the conversation. In either case, it will help you keep the meeting on track and it also acts usefully to help you keep things straight in your own mind. Keep people with you in this way; it can help keep them with you right up to the moment they say "yes".

## Showing as well as telling

In the world of selling, a "sales aid" is any physical element used to enhance what is said and make an explanation clearer or a point more powerful. Here we consider the use of this sort of thing in a wider context and, if "sales aid" is an inappropriate description let's call them "case enhancers", because that is what they are intended to do. But first, consider – how do you store them? In a word: carefully. So many times I have seen people who have either not been able to find something they have said they will show and which they intend to use to add weight to an argument, or who have pulled an item from a bulging file that looks as if it contains the aftermath of a small explosion; hardly the way to appear professional. Such inefficiency will be noticed and all such aids are important – they deserve to be looked after.

Any case enhancer deserves to be used correctly and the golden rule is simple; you must let them speak for themselves. If there are two things many people find difficult in meetings, they are being patient and keeping silent. And the good use of aids demands both. For example, imagine that presentation again. You are trying to persuade your colleague that a common style for the slides you both use is appropriate. You have an example of what you mean, but their use still demands a systematic approach:

- The specimen slides must first be introduced. This introduction should explain why they are being shown, in other words what it will help explain – and why they will find it helpful.
- Then you show them. And you wait while they look at them. You wait until their attention comes back to you from the slides because, if the thing is of any interest at all, then when it is put in front of them they will want to look at it, will do just that and doing so will take their attention.
- No one can look at something, concentrate on it, and listen to you at the same time. So you wait. And the more complex or the more interesting something you show them proves, the longer you must remain waiting silently. This may seem a simple point, but because it can seem awkward to keep silent there is a great temptation to chip in and continue the conversation.
- But if you do, and if what you say makes an important point, you may succeed only in distracting from the visual image and yet not do so sufficiently for someone to take in the point you have just made. After a moment's hiatus the conversation resumes and not as good a total point has been made as you would have wished.
- This scenario is made more complicated if you have, say, complicated plans to go through: every time you turn over a page you must wait for them to take in what they see and for their attention to return to you before you continue talking.
- Then you remove it, so that it does not distract as you continue speaking (you can promise to leave a copy, come back to it, or whatever is appropriate) and continue the conversation.

The effect of seeing something during a conversation is powerful. It makes things easier to understand. And when it does, this, of course, is likely to be noticed and valued. It helps paint a picture, and it can save time – again a commodity that many people will doubtless value. It also adds variety to the meeting and this too helps maintain concentration.

Furthermore, such items can appear personalised. Something may be shown as what is clearly part of standard material and there is nothing wrong with that – it will be expected if such a thing is logical and someone may well like what they see and find it useful. But there is sometimes an opportunity for material to create a different impression by being (or sometimes seeming to be) tailored just for this one occasion.

Back to the slides: you could show some well matched ones from something else, or actually prepare a couple in the style you are commending for the presentation in question. Often if someone sees that something has been provided specially for them, they appreciate it more. It does not simply help explain; it can act to develop and build the relationship between the two parties.

Well used, items like this can make people find a meeting or conversation memorable. It pays dividends to make sure that you have an adequate number of them, that they are good quality and appropriate – that they are genuinely helpful to people – and to use them carefully and effectively.

Note: So important is it to get things right in this area – the right aids, appropriately organised – that in any repetitive situation you may find it useful to list what you plan to use on a checklist. Listing the items you have to deploy, linking them to such factors as:

- The situation they best relate to.
- What aspect of what you will say they illustrate.
- Proof that what you say is true.

Remember that anything can be used. I once met a sales engineer who sold mining equipment (drills the size of a small car); in meetings he produced from a large pilot case a large, extremely heavy chunk of rock. One side of it was cut as when a knife goes through butter into a shiny flat surface, and he had a wonderful tale about the rock being the hardest granite in the world. It certainly made a point to anyone not able to descend a mine shaft and inspect his equipment in situ. When you think what you might use in this kind of way cast your net wide, think creatively and exclude nothing that might help.

## Avoid exaggeration

This is a most important maxim. Never, ever exaggerate. Nothing switches people off more quickly than obvious exaggeration; do not be tempted to do it. One phrase too many and your credibility collapses around you; in fact of all the mistakes you can make in persuasion this is certainly... you are right, I am exaggerating – but to make a useful point!

More seriously, credibility is a fragile flower and a good case can very easily be diluted by something that positions you as going "over the top". If you have a good case by all means say so, but give reasons for excellence and spend your time talking more about what something does for or means to someone than about simply the fact that it is good.

Beware particularly of superlatives. If you say something is "the best" then you must be able to back it up. Too strident a description from which you have to climb down, "Well, when I say best, I mean undoubtedly one of the best ..." will dilute any good impression you may initially have achieved. Remember the scepticism with which much of what anyone with "something to sell" is received, and that people may well question each statement, asking themselves whether it should be taken at face value, whether it is to be believed and deciding whether the overall case being presented is becoming stronger or weaker.

Finally, remember also – a common mistake – that few things are "unique" (a much overused word meaning literally like nothing else). This means that usually saying something is quite, very or entirely "unique" is simply incorrect and a misuse of a useful word, one which can be powerful when correctly used. There is a chance here too that some people will notice such mistakes and not take on board the positive points that are being made; again diluting effectiveness.

## Avoid pressurising people

People like to make considered judgments. Pressure to make a decision before they have completed what they regard as the necessary thinking process, weighing up the pros and cons of a potential decision, will often have the reverse effect of that desired. It will increase their resolve to think it through and not to be rushed. People usually read undue pressure in three ways, as:

- Insensitivity to their point of view (this is particularly bad because one of the things they often positively seek as a characteristic of someone they respect is an understanding of them and their point of view).
- A smoke screen, at worst one specifically designed to disguise some weakness in your case, which you apparently feel will show itself in time; hence the inappropriate rush to close the deal.
- Desperation, which might have all sorts of causes – none of which inspire confidence, or make you appear anything but unprofessional.

So go for a successful outcome by all means, push hard, be persistent and have and display the courage of your convictions, but do not put undue pressure on people in a way that will be obvious and which will be read as unprofessional, especially if doing so is an alternative to using the more positive techniques discussed here. Be particularly careful of this when there is a genuine need to hurry.

### Add a demonstration
If appropriate, an effective demonstration can strengthen what is said considerably, and is another area to potentially heighten differentiation. Seeing is believing. There is no substitute for someone actually having the evidence of their own eyes to back up what is said to them. Imagine being told about some new system to be run on your computer without seeing anything of how it would work. Demonstrations certainly add power, but must be approached in the right way; they must be effective and that means 100% effective. Anything less simply does not meet the need.

An effective demonstration starts with prior consideration of the demonstration's audience. It may be to one person; it may be to several. A group situation illustrates some of the problems of a formal presentation. You may feel exposed standing in front of an expectant group, and thinking beforehand about what you will say and how you will make it go smoothly; and in a way that will boost your self-confidence. Each person may have a different agenda and be looking for, and potentially swayed by, different points. So, depending on who is involved and what their situation, current experience and knowledge of something is, you need to proceed so as to make your demonstration effective. Thus you should:

- Have everything ready and set up.
- Make everything seen and heard 100% clear.
- Ensure what you do works!
- Involve people: make them feel how it could be for them.
- Give a precise emphasis (for example if you want to stress how quickly something must be done – make it quick and make them notice).

During the whole process the emphasis should be on proof. You are not just talking about it, you can show it and they can try or experience it. You must work to ensure this and everything else you say and do is done just as you believe is best. There are very few second chances in persuasion and that should condition your thinking. Time spent beforehand to make sure that you get everything right is time very well spent.

## MAXIMISING YOUR CHANCES
As is no doubt clear by now, everything helps; as was said earlier success is, at least in part, in the details. So before moving on let me mention three more factors that can strengthen your approach.

### No me, me, me
You might say that setting out to get agreement involves an egocentric approach. You have to think of it as your meeting, you want – indeed intend – it to be successful, you have to go for the objective, and that is always ultimately to obtain agreement so that you get your own way. All true and necessary, yet this approach should not show inappropriately and must not show overtly in your language.

So, do not prefix things you say by, for example: *If you want my opinion* ..., or *If I were you I would* .... It too easily sounds patronising (and reminds me of the worst kind of boss saying, *When I want your opinion, I'll give it to you.* Sorry, I digress). People may well be interested in your advice, but they expect it to be relevant to them, and based on some real consideration of their circumstances. Much better to lead into comments with something like: *For someone in your position the best approach is often* ..., or *Given what you said about timing, we might best deal with it by* ....

People want to know, and to recognise clearly, that you are acting on their behalf and that what you say has their interests in mind; your opinion in isolation they can do without. You will find a conscious line of avoiding egocentric sounding phraseology gives the best impression, and helps position you as someone of some weight.

## Be loyal to others

When you represent an entity of some sort – an organisation, a department, even a committee – you will win acceptance more easily if people have not only a good relationship with you, but also a good image of whatever it is that you represent. In the world of business, many firms spend a great deal of money creating a good background image through public relations, design and other techniques. It is easy to undo this good work in a moment.

Consider: in the course of a discussion you are faced with a complaint because of a missed deadline. Imagine too that it was not your fault, but that, for whatever reason, it has understandably caused upset. Everyone is concerned to protect their own personal image and reputation and it is easy to find yourself saying something along the lines of: "You will appreciate it was out of my hands, I don't know how many times I have told those people how important it is to meet timing commitments, but they still seem to have got it wrong ..." If you have to then say this again, the damage is made worse, and in either case the other person is left feeling that however good their contact with you, the people or organisation behind you is less than efficient. What may have been intended to bolster your image ends up doing the reverse, when just saying, "I'm sorry" might have worked much better (saying so does not necessarily imply acceptance of personal blame if you simple speak on

68

behalf of a body or organisation of some sort).

You may on occasion need to support policy set by others (even when you disapprove of it), defend colleagues who are less efficient than yourself and positively work at building the image of whoever you represent. People may well understand that no organisation is perfect, but one that seems to hold itself in low regard is seen as dubious – "If that is all they think of themselves", they may think, "how can I have confidence in what they will do for me?" It is easy to let the wrong kind of description slip through and, if it becomes a habit, then the damage may be considerable.

Boost the image of others at every opportunity, even when you have to sort out difficulties; it can smooth the path for what follows and make what you do in persuasion just a little more certain. In this position you need to take it on the chin: "We do seem to have fallen down there, let's see ..." commenting in a way that does not seem to be you avoiding blame and moving quickly on to what can be done to put things right.

## Offer more

Here, if you represent an organisation of some sort, then you may be dependent on company or central policy and have to take that into account in terms of what you offer. Yet the principle here is an important and powerful aid to increasing the power of the case you make, so it deserves a mention.

You can increase the likelihood of success by offering more: more than usual, more than someone else, more than expected, and this applies to both tangible and intangible things. Many of the ways that spring to mind are temporary (they have less impact once they are permanent and taken for granted) and, with a business hat on, might be best described as promotional. We are all familiar with this sort of thing as we shop. As an example, retailers may offer:

- A free sample or trial of something.
- Some free element of product (like a free first chapter of an e-book).
- Limited or exclusive offer.
- Saving, avoiding a coming price increase, an additional one-off

discount, and more (one particular form of this has entered the language – the 'bogof': 'Buy One Get One Free').

- Higher specification for the cost of the basic offering.
- Incentive (a gift, a trip, a competition).
- Trade-in allowance for upgrading what is bought.
- Better than usual credit terms.
- Special guarantee.
- Discounts or other rewards linked to future purchase.

Intangible factors may be involved here too. For instance, people: a professional firm might promise to put John in as project leader as he worked with you successfully previously. A past customer might not doubt the competencies of others but still prefer to work with someone they know and trust. Although such things are by no means applicable or appropriate on every occasion, any of these and more can act to increase the likelihood of success. Generally, such devices act in a number of different ways, they:

- Help you get a hearing, perhaps for the first time.
- Help improve the weight of the case you can present.
- Can pull commitment forward, persuading people to agree now rather than later.
- Can increase the size of a commitment.
- Can affect the frequency of agreement.

They can also have negative effects, reducing the seeming importance of other benefits; or, in retailing, encouraging people to shop around, and only buy in turn from whoever is currently offering the best deal (and we know this occurs – we all do it to some extent).

Any offer must form an organised, integrated part of your case. For a company such promotional offers must link to marketing strategy as they can affect image and profitability and cash flow. Some you may feel would work well in your situation, in which case you may want to incorporate them into what you do. Such ploys are undeniably useful, but you should never rely on them to the exclusion of making a sound case for agreement in other ways.

## Pen to paper

While being persuasive, in terms of its individual elements, is pretty much common sense, there is more than enough to it to create some real complexity. Something that certainly complicates matters is when a persuasive message must be put in writing: into a letter (or e-mail) or some longer document. Further detail, certainly about making the language persuasive, is beyond our brief here, though I have written at greater length about it in a business context: see *Effective Business Writing* (Kogan Page). The most important thing is to keep it simple and favourable: short words, short sentences and short paragraphs. Do not let phrases become unnecessarily verbose, for instance writing 'At this moment in time' when you mean now, and remember to use sufficient punctuation so that your reader can both read and breathe.

Thought the details are beyond our brief here, do remember that anything you must put in writing is only going to be persuasive if it is first well written and well expressed. Putting things in writing and doing so poorly will always dilute effectiveness and may make a message seem stilted. Always approach written things with care and aim for real precision. Remember that written messages last – and may come back to haunt you later, sometimes much later.

Here in the core of the persuasive conversation there is clearly a good deal to think about (hence the long chapter); furthermore, even if you get all this right and things are going well, there can still be other problems. People may listen carefully, nod encouragingly, but still raise objections. There is so often a "but" and the next chapter shows how to respond.

# Chapter 5

# RESISTENCE IS FUTILE
# Handling and overcoming objections

'Obstacles are made to be overcome.'
*Proverb*

A well presented case may of course result in instant agreement and there is no more to be done. If so, great; but often, though all seems be going well and you feel you are making an unarguable case, when you pause hoping for agreement the first thing you hear starts with the little word, 'But'. Let us be clear: objections are an inherent part of any kind of persuasive process.

---

**KEY DIFFERENTIATING FACTORS:**
Let's put this right up front: *welcome objections, handling them well can be impressive and act to move you successfully towards agreement.*

---

They spring directly from the human nature involved in what is being done and, whatever you are doing, you can be sure there will likely be some. When people raise them it is not necessarily a sign that there is any problem, indeed it can be a positive sign of some interest on their part. By and large people do not bother taking time to query things when they have no interest in the overall case whatsoever. There is an old saying that: 'he who findeth fault meaneth to buy' – quite so. So handling objections is an inherent part of the process. If this part is done well it does not only redress the balance, or remove the objection entirely, its being well handled will itself be impressive.

People like dealing with other people whom, as they might put it, "know their stuff". The smooth handling of objections is taken as a sign of confidence and competence. Not that you will always be able to remove them. There is no merit in trying to persuade people that black is white if it is, in fact, as black as pitch (or even if it is distinctly grey), and the last thing you want is to prompt an argument.

Rebalancing is what counts, as the points in this chapter describe.

## THINK POSITIVE

Some people say objections are a sign of interest, and this is certainly a good way to regard them. Certainly you should expect to receive them. As we have seen, the way people go about making decisions is to weigh up the pros and cons. They expect to find some things on the downside (think of going to the shops: few things we buy are perfect; indeed we would be suspicious if something is so described!). You should watch, however, for the quantity of objections you get. Too many can be a sign that it is your fault. By this I mean that with experience you will know roughly how much objection will be raised in a given situation, and to some extent what issues are likely to be involved. If you find that someone in a kind of persuasive encounter that you have regularly is raising more objections than you expect, then it may be that you:

- Have failed to identify sufficiently accurately what their situation and perception is and that what you are saying is therefore off target. More questions may correct this.
- Are making suggestions too soon. People who feel their situation is unique or who expect a tailored recommendation may feel that what you are saying should follow more thought about them on your part.
- May (albeit inadvertently) be giving the impression of a set, standard presentation, when this will put people off. Often it is not credible that something should be regarded as being all things to all people. Everyone wants you to relate what you describe to

them individually, not simply go through some seemingly standard "patter"; thus for a manager there may be many good reasons for people to take on a project, but what may best persuade one individual is a particular selection and arrangement of them.

In all these cases observation may allow you to spot what is happening and to adjust your approach in a way that minimises the problem. If necessary you can jump back to earlier in the conversation: "I get the distinct impression that I haven't explained this very well, what I should have said was …" This effectively allows you to have a second chance, revisiting part of your explanation and aiming to make it more powerful so that it no longer prompts a but.

So, objections can help keep you on track, they are a sign of interest and can also be an opportunity to impress people by the way you deal with things (not, of course, that you should encourage objections just so that you can impressively demolish them!). When they do occur, however, and they will, there is no reason why you cannot regard them as something routine and something where how you handle them can act to build your credibility. Well handled they can become final stepping-stones en route to the far bank and a successful agreement.

## PREVENTING OBJECTIONS

Prevention being better than cure is a sound principle. In objection handling there are two ways in which prevention can help.

First consider the area of preparation. Few objections should come at you like a bolt from the blue; most of the topics of objection that occur you will have anticipated if you have thought things through or, with a regular topic, you may well have had to deal with previously. Specific circumstances create examples: if you are trying to involve someone in a project and it will involve them in some public speaking, then, given that many people are wary of doing this, you might anticipate objections (if that is you, then see another book in this series, *Presentations* by Frances Kay).

You should have thought through any perennial objections you receive or, on a one-off situation, anticipate receiving and, although they will often be phrased in different ways and come with different power and emphasis, you should be ready for them and have various ways of handling them in mind. As and when new, or differently phrased, objections do occur, you need to think about possible answers to these too and add something about them to your repertoire.

Secondly, there are objections that may typically remain unspoken. This does not mean they are not in peoples' minds; some will be and these will then go to form part of the balance upon which they will ultimately agree or reject your proposition. Where experience shows that this is likely to be happening it may be necessary for you to raise the issue yourself in order to deal with a specific point and get it out of the frame. This is best approached head on: *You may have been wondering about ... let me spend a minute explaining how we can deal with that ... You have not mentioned ... do you have any questions about that?* And if you have thought through the answer, or at least the kind of answer necessary, then you can deal with the matter and perhaps also make it seem reasonably inconsequential.

## HANDLING OBJECTIONS
Two stages are important.

### "Sparring" with objections
Objections cannot always be demolished; we are not even always able to overcome them and we certainly do not want objection handling to develop into an argument. Indeed it is quite possible to win an argument, yet lose the chance of coming to an agreement. If, when someone raises an objection, you immediately allow your hackles to rise and your every response to seem like instant rebuttal starting with the words, *Ah, but* ..., there is every chance that the conversation will become a tad confrontational and that is not conducive to gaining agreement. It is for this reason that you should use the technique known as "sparring". Sparring offers an appropriate initial response and is a useful preliminary to the process of objection handling and providing a satisfactory answer. Such sparring can do several things; it acts to make it clear that you:

● Are listening carefully.
● Will initiate no argument.

- Accept the point made and will deal with it rather than deny it.
- Will treat what has been said seriously.
- Do not think the objection is contentious, or unnecessarily demanding.

So, sparring is the process of saying something that positions how you will deal with the objection: *That's a good point John, I can see I must give you more information in that area ...*, *You are quite right to raise that, it is an important point, let me ...*, preferably something that includes – or better still starts with – at least a hint of agreement. In this way you can provoke feelings in the objector's mind that will make dealing with the objection easier.

This can mean starting boldly with the word "Yes", even when you know what you want to do next is persuade someone they are wrong. Because doing so is counter intuitive, it needs remembering and may also necessitate a conscious effort. However, if you can make someone say to themselves: "Good, there's not going to be an argument" or "They accept the point, now let's see what they have to say about it" then they will be more receptive to what you say next. This principle may be more important than it seems because some objection areas are difficult and can quickly become emotional. Sparring has the effect of "lowering the temperature" of the conversation prior to going on to provide the answer.

This technique helps in another way. Sometimes you will get objections that are new, that you are not expecting, not familiar with or that do, if only for a moment, throw you. These can present real difficulty when you feel you have to come back fast with a credible response and leave no hiatus in the conversation. Luckily, the construction of the human mind is such that in the time it will take you to say something like: "That's a good point, Mary, we are certainly going to have to satisfy you about that if we're to reach agreement. Let me ...", then your mind can be doing a great deal of thinking and you may well be on the way to an answer.

Sparring builds in a bit of time to think just when you may need it most; and very useful that can be too, especially as it allows it to happen without pointing up the fact that you need it. It sets up a situation that is as favourable as possible to dealing with the objection itself, and makes it more likely that you can do so effectively.

But, ultimately, you still have to answer the point made.

### ... Providing an answer

Never attempt to deal with an objection until you have sufficient information as to exactly where someone is coming from as the basis of your answering. If you assume wrongly exactly what is meant, or treat a serious point superficially, you will quickly be in trouble and likely to make matters worse. Objections must not be allowed to put you on the defensive. Sparring helps set the scene. Two other initial responses are also well worth bearing in mind.

First, never be afraid to respond to a question with a question of your own. This will be understood and accepted, after all how can you be expected to comment sensibly about a point until you know exactly what lies behind it? More than one question may be quite acceptable, though you should make it clear what you are doing: "That's a fair point, John, let me make sure I understand exactly what you mean; can you tell me ...". This is an important point as simple questions or comments may either disguise a deeper point or, more often, can have several possible interpretations.

Consider an example in a sales situation, or indeed anything where agreement demands expenditure. A customer may comment on price or a manager on costs (they so often do!), saying something like: "That is very expensive". What do they mean? It is a comment, it's not even phrased as a question, and could mean many things; for instance, it could mean:

- "It is more than I expected."
- "It is more than I pay now."
- "It is more than another quote".
- "It is over my budget."
- "That cost is beyond my authority to decide."
- "I'm not convinced it is value for money."
- "Will you negotiate?"
- "I'm not clear what I get for it."
- "It is a lot to pay at once."
- "I don't understand."

- "No."
- "Can the (product) specification be reduced to cut costs?"
- "I will have to think about that."
- "I cannot decide now."

You may think of more such meanings. Clearly, many of these interpretations will need answering along different lines; it makes the point clearly that you always have to understand exactly what is meant before you deal with it. This is true of so many things: persuading someone to serve on a committee might well get them saying, "I can't afford the time". But that too needs qualifying: at present/on the regular meeting day? Or maybe it's just a polite way of putting you off – if someone cannot drive and is worried about the journey to the meeting they may avoid the issues that raises. Even the busiest person might be prepared to rearrange things to some extent if they feel it is worthwhile.

Secondly, if something is thrown out as a comment or challenge, just like "that is very expensive" in the above example, and it is in a form that is not a question, then you can often turn it back to the questioner as a question designed to clarify. Thus: "But that is very expensive" could be followed by the question: "Yes, Mary, it is a considerable cost, though I would suggest, of course, it is a good investment. But what exactly are you saying? Is it more than you had budgeted for?" This kind of approach does a number of things quickly; it:

- Acknowledges the point. (Note here that there is no merit in denying it is a great deal of money if they clearly feel that it is; indeed there is no merit in any argument that is merely about personal and subjective judgements.)
- Suggests you will be pleased to discuss it.
- Makes asking for more information about their concern seem helpful.

Once these preliminaries are out of the way, you can move on to actually address the objection. If you continue to keep in mind the image of a balance (described earlier) and bear in mind that there will be points – of varying importance and weight, on either side – then the job you must do here is one of ordering the balance, or reordering the one you have described, so that – despite some objections – it still presents a favourable basis for a positive decision. Often, of course, people are not going to automatically agree just because the balance is positive, they are only going to agree if your described balance stacks up better than those of any alternative which they may also be evaluating.

Ultimately, as you answer objections, you have only four options that you can use in rebalancing, so at least mechanistically there is no great complication here. You can only:

- **Remove them:** the first option is to remove the objection, to persuade the person that it is not actually a negative factor. Often objections arise out of sheer confusion, for example when the presenting partner said "I don't have time for a full rehearsal!" This might be based on an overestimate of how long it will take. If so, tell them what you have in mind is an hour or so, and not the whole morning they envisaged, and the objection evaporates.
- **Reduce them:** or you can act to show that although there is a negative element to the case, it is a minor matter – "Getting this presentation right is so important, it will take a moment certainly, but surely an hour or so is worthwhile?"
- **Turn them into a plus:** here you take what seems like a negative factor and show that it is, in fact, the opposite – "Rehearsal seems elaborate and it will take an hour or so, but we both have to do some individual preparation. Rehearsal will halve that time and ensure the presentation goes well."
- **Agree:** the last option, and one that the facts sometimes make necessary, is to agree that an objection raised is a snag – "You're right, it is time-consuming, but this presentation has to go well and there is no other option."

As these are the only alternatives, once you have decided if the objection is real, imagined or based on incorrect understanding, you simply have to choose what suits best in a particular case. In all cases, especially perhaps the last, your answer can link back to benefits, touching again on points made earlier in a way that can act as a summary and prompt people to consider the whole balance rather than one point in isolation.

## Money problems

Money is often a sensitive issue. We do not want to be ripped off. We love a bargain and generally want to be sure that any figures that are suggested to us make sense. In the business world, careful description of price will minimise the incidence of price objections. Careful handling of them will remove what can often be a major obstacle to agreement; for those readers for whom this is relevant, this is worth a separate mention. So skip on if you like, though the principles involved here could be applied to other objections that involve figures and money. Even at the simple a level of persuading someone to take a break and lunch out, the question "How much?" may well crop up.

Certainly in selling situations, of all the things that come up as objections this is often the most frequent and the most difficult. Of course, everyone wants value for money, and in many areas they will negotiate to get it if they can. Negotiation is an additional skill and body of techniques to that of selling: if selling – persuasion – obtains agreement, then negotiation agrees the details of that agreement. Negotiation techniques are dealt with in a separate book in this series (*Negotiation* by Anthony Jacks), but to give you a flavour, such techniques always remind me of a quotation – Annabel (aged six) saying: "If you want a guinea pig then you start by asking for a pony." A girl with some inherent understanding it seems; but I digress.

At the least customers want to assess value for money and often to compare what is offered in this respect with competition or other options. So how can this be handled? Let us continue to focus on sales situations here for a moment more. First, the way someone positions a statement of price has an effect on the likelihood of subsequently receiving price objections. Price should rarely be dealt with in isolation, by describing it alongside benefits you can make it speak much more of value for money. This certainly applies for any factor likely to be contentious.

People, perhaps especially sales people, must beware also of presenting price (or costs) so that it runs foul of the way in which people regard money psychologically. For example:

- **Avoid price barriers:** we all see things priced at sums like £9.99 in many retail outlets, and somehow this is perceived as being significantly less than something at £10. Similarly, with higher amounts, £4,995 seems less than £5,000, a house priced at £259,500 is set below the nearest round figure (and tax thresholds complicate this further). This may seem silly to you; we all know such figures are virtually the same thing as the round figure above them, but there is a great deal of research to back up the psychological response to such things – the lower price really does mean agreement to buy is more likely. I suggest you do not worry about why, but use the fact where you can.

- **Amortise price:** this is the technique of quoting a figure of, say, £1,000 (or around a thousand) per month, which seems less than £12,000 over a year. This can be used in a variety of ways to split larger figures down, spreading them over different budgets, people, or time frames. The amounts do not have to be large: breaking £50.00 a year down and saying that it is less than a pound a week may be equally worthwhile. Additionally, any way of stressing the economies of scale is also part of this.

If you have more flexibility in setting prices, as is the case with those selling a tailored service (as I do in training), for example, then:

- **Judge price range carefully:** to say something will be between £4,000 and £7,000 may seem too vague, whereas £4,000 – £5,000 or even £5,500 may be acceptable as a first ballpark figure. A second point here: always be careful about the highest point of a range. Quote something you then exceed and the perception of you changes for the worse and does so fast: "These people always go over their estimate". Coming in below an estimate helps ensure people are sufficiently satisfied to come back to you next time
- **Avoid round figures:** when quoting bespoke arrangements, as is again the case with consultancy and fees, with the work based on the client's unique brief, it will not be credible if it comes to a round figure like £10,000. If it does, people will assume that this is an impossible coincidence and probably also that you have worked out a figure and then rounded it up.

This applies too to costing an internal project, and whenever price and costs are involved you should use language carefully to minimise (or maximise) the effect they engender as required.

A final point on this: perhaps more than anywhere else, objections based on money factors in all their manifestations are things for which you must be ready. Prepare well and deal with them with authority and confidence and you will find you can handle them.

**Respect alternative choices**
If someone is not just deciding yes or no, but choosing between alternative propositions, you may well be aware of this fact. If you want someone to spend time on rehearsing a presentation (back to that example) and they say they have a report to finish writing, you immediately suggesting that doing so is not important will not be likely to go down very well.

So do not knock alternatives. This is certainly good advice for someone selling a product or service (here the alternatives are competitors). Sometimes, sales people will be asked outright about competition: "what about firm X?" Or: "we also plan to talk to company Y, do you know them?" If you are in this position, two responses are to be avoided: do not:

- **Single them out:** "Yes, I know them; they are my biggest competitor." Such a response is likely to make the buyer think they should check them out
- **Knock them:** "I certainly know them; I thought everyone knew the trouble they are having in the market at present." It is just life that at that point they declare that they have done business together very satisfactorily in the past, or that there is some other connection that makes such a knock particularly inappropriate. Besides, it is very difficult not to let such comments sound like sour grapes.

More constructive responses are called for, something like: "There are a dozen or more competitors for us in this sector; we come across them all and each has certain strengths." This makes checking them all out seem complicated and, while giving no detail, does acknowledge that you know they are also good. This is also a more credible response.

Exactly the same kind of thing may occurs across a wide range of situations. If you are fundraising for a charity, you may find people are reluctant to contribute because they say, "I already support X". Try to persuade your son to mow the lawn and you will not get far by knocking the things (many things no doubt) that he has to do that prevent it. Acceptance that the other things are important may well be a better starting point and then the job is to show reasons why this chore should still be fitted in (a little more persuasion might save some money here given the attitude of many teenagers!).

Care in all references to any sort of competitive offering or alternative always pays off; the last thing you want is a protracted argument, prompted by some detailed negative comment you make. Someone may then feel they must defend their position, as accepting it may make their past decision about something else look ill-judged.

One last point here" if a "competitor" is named (and you can do worse than ask if they are not) then information about what you are up against may well help you decide on the line you will take. A manager who is just too busy is much more difficult to persuade than the one who tells you specifically what he feels he should be doing rather than investigating your suggested project.

## Apples and oranges

It is said that while you can compare apples with apples, there is no merit in comparing apples with old shoes. Yet people do the latter all the time. Customers say something like: "That's all very well but I can get the same thing from Firm X on much better terms" to sales people. Though usually what they actually mean is that they can get something rather different from elsewhere; otherwise they would surely not be debating the point; they would simply go elsewhere. On that basis they are no doubt correct – there are always many permutations on offer in any particular industry. They seek justification of a particular package or deal, and very often of the price (they may want a discount), in comparison with the alternative – though they rarely elaborate on the details of that other offering.

The answer in such circumstances cannot lie with a direct comparison when, as is most often the case, the two things are not in any case exactly the same. This is true of many situations: someone might contrast spending time on a committee by saying I can spend the time just as usefully in another way. But it will not be the same. A sales person's quoted competitor may be less costly, but the specification may also be less, the quality lower, fewer ancillary items may be included, associated costs may be higher, credit terms or guarantees may be different, design details may vary, delivery or timing may be longer or less certain. The possibilities are many.

Persuasive responses must identify and then deal with these differences. The first answer may well be, "Yes, you can get something similar elsewhere," (do not deny it, that way lies fruitless argument) "but it is certainly not identical; in our discussions you have emphasised the need for reliability, our ..." and go back to the specific benefits you have identified they want. In some circumstances your first response may need to be a question; you have to find out more about what is being offered to discover how in fact it differs from your offering.

In terms of the price of a product, if one is more expensive then the additional amount over and above a competitor can only be explained and justified by reference to the gap between what the two parties offer; in other words what does the extra amount of money buy? Does it provide better service, higher quality, or what? Or indeed what would paying less lead them to miss; for you can discuss it both ways round. Identifying and dealing with this gap is the route to answering any objection that comes up from this sort of lead in.

People certainly want value for money, they also want a "good deal", but they will not sacrifice key requirements for savings or reductions in other factors (quality etc.) that may prove to be a false economy. It is a fact that many of the most successful products and services in many markets are not the cheapest; just look at the big name products in supermarkets. Cost and quality go together; and so if money is involved in what you are doing you should describe your quality or "value" with confidence; it is what justifies the cost.

Avoid odious and inappropriate comparisons, which people may make only to antagonise, or as an opening to negotiation, and make sure that, whatever someone else may do, you only ever compare apples with apples.

## "Boomerang" technique

Something else that can be useful in handling objections is a particular form of words, which turns an objection back on itself so that the question posed links to the answer. Thus:

**John:** "As you know this is now very urgent, I don't know that we have time for …".
**Mary:** "It is because I know you want things sorted out fast, John, that I am suggesting this. It will not take long and could avoid more significant delays if you went ahead without and hit any snags".

If the topic here is linked to something that someone rates highly, such as needing something urgently, then this kind of response can get you back on track away from the difficulties and apparently focusing on exactly what they see as important. This technique constitutes a manner of presentation that can make someone feel that what they regard as the key issue is genuinely being acknowledged, and that the answer is being dealt with in a way that addresses it.

### Just an excuse

Let us be honest, sometimes people disguise their reasons for not acting as we wish. They say – it will take too long – the cost is too great – or whatever else when they are simply being stubborn or are unwilling for whatever reason to say exactly what they think (and this could be to save your feelings!). In this case you need to try to recognise what is an excuse and what is not. A long justification of time or cost will achieve nothing if that is only a disguise for the real reason. For example, say your fellow presenter said they did not like the thought of presenting with you. Maybe what they are saying is that they are not very confident of their presentational skills and do not want you to witness or surpass them.

Suspect something like this is going on and the only way forward is to ask questions, and perhaps to drive things out in the open – "Be honest, that's not really an issue. Why do you really object?"

### Saving face

Peoples' objections sometimes prove false. Something makes them challenge some point when actually the facts are entirely on your side and the balance is positive. The temptation in a hectic meeting, especially one in which a fair number of objections have been raised, including perhaps some difficult ones, is to heave a sigh of relief that one is mistaken and blurt out the equivalent of "You're wrong!" This is a natural reaction but can result in the instigator of the point being made to feel bad, or worse, feeling they have been made to look silly. Clearly this is something to be avoided if good relations are to be maintained.

There can be many reasons for people to be mistaken; an original impression about something you have told them may be wrong, out-of-date perhaps. They may have misheard something or misinterpreted something they read, or it could be your fault – you may have put something over badly, not gone into sufficient detail, gone on talking while their attention was elsewhere. Or you may not know where the fault lies; indeed it may not matter.

It's important here to let people down lightly. Suggest that it is an easy or commonly-made mistake. This may still leave them feeling somewhat bad. It may be better than this to suggest you are at fault, albeit in a general and unspecified way: "Sorry, perhaps I gave you the wrong impression about that, the fact is ...", "If I was insufficiently clear about that, I apologise, it is not, in fact, a problem; the fact is ..."

This works well in either case. Sometimes people know, or realise, they are at fault and rather like an approach that avoids laying blame or making them feel bad about it. Sometimes it's no one's fault, but the approach is still seen to be sensitive. Just a little care in this area can get over what otherwise can be small upsets to the smooth progress of the conversation and the development of a positive case. You should not overdo it, or it will risk sounding patronising, but do avoid drawing attention to errors.

All this – the smooth, assured handling of peoples' objections – is an important one to get to grips with, one to be regarded as an opportunity. Not least it avoids there being any hiatus between the presentation of a strong case and the next stage, that of obtaining a firm, positive commitment.

# Chapter 6

# CLOSING
# Tying down an agreement

'The only sure thing is that there are no sure things.'
*Akio Morita (Sony)*

The need to "close" (the sales jargon word used for securing agreement) is perhaps what sets persuasive communication apart from other more straightforward kinds of communication. It can involve getting the other person to make a decision, change their minds or even upturn the habits of a lifetime. As such it can present problems. The whole process is psychologically difficult in some senses for whoever is doing the persuading, holding out as it does the prospect of success – or failure and a lack of agreement. Furthermore, people sometimes find it difficult to make a decision. It is a stage that is dependent on what has gone before, but it is also one that must occur of itself.

If you cannot or will not actually ask for agreement, perhaps through a fear of rejection, then your overall effectiveness will always be less powerful than it might otherwise be. Here we review this crucial stage.

## MAKING A COMMITMENT
Gaining agreement is the ultimate objective of all persuasion. Sometimes the nature of a particular persuasive process means that you can reach it in stages, in which case you effectively have to close a

number of times, on all the interim commitments, of which there can be many. It may represent a close to get someone to say a number of things, for example:

- Yes, I'll meet with you.
- Yes, send something (perhaps some documentation).
- Yes, let me have a detailed proposal.
- Yes, let's meet again to take things further.
- Yes, I agree (the ultimate decision).

The final attempt to gain a commitment is less a full stage of the process (in the sense of the time it takes); rather it is often just a phrase or, more often, merely a question. You have to know when to ask such a question and you have to actually do it.

Closing can be a weak area with some persuaders, one that allows previous good case making to be wasted as agreement is not made to conclude the process. Indeed sometimes the fault is that little or nothing is done to prompt it, though that may be less because it is done badly, than because it is not done at all.

Some – most? – people, understandably dislike it when people say "No" – and in some circumstances this may not be said politely. So they are tempted and may find themselves taking a safer route to ending a conversation. They say things like: "I hope this has been useful" – "I hope I have been able to give you all the details you need at this stage" – "Is there anything else I can add before we finish?"

This kind of non-close finish almost guarantees a pleasant end to the meeting, making it easy for people to respond with statements such as: "That's been very useful, thanks very much for talking to me" – "You've given me all the information I need at this stage, thank you very much for your time." All very nice, everyone likes to feel they have been helpful and everyone likes to receive thanks; but such responses are usually followed by two other little words: "Good Bye", drawing matters to an end before a commitment has been made and before any follow-up action can be arranged.

You must therefore resolve to close – to actually ask for agreement. You have to be thick-skinned about any rejection; even the most persuasive people do not have a 100% strike rate, so there will always be some negative conclusions (though some can perhaps be recovered later). But if you aim to close every time at every stage, then, along with a little rejection, you may well get more successful agreements than those who approach it in a more faint heart manner.

## MANAGING THE CLOSING PROCESS

The best time to go for a commitment is often said to be at the earliest moment possible. This is a little glib, but there is some truth in it, to the extent that you can leave things too late and allow the moment to pass. Certainly you need to watch for signs that someone is ready to make a decision.

Left alone some people are very indecisive, or at the least they will take a long time to make up their minds. This may be for constructive reasons, and you must be wary of trying to shortcut the weighing up factors, which they see as making a sensible decision possible; people are very wary of being rushed into something. But if the delay is just out of what some people might see as a perverse desire to delay, then closing may act as a catalyst to prompt a decision.

Note that this final stage does not cause people to agree. Only the power of persuasion from the picture you have built up and the case you have put over can do that – by creating the interest that closing then converts into becoming a positive agreement. So, the final kind of feedback you need during a persuasive conversation is in the form of what (in selling) are called "buying signals".

These signals of agreement are less easy to define than to spot. Some will be in the form of a series of signs of interest, expressions, comments, noises even, nods certainly, all of which indicate satisfaction with what is being presented. The most tangible sign is probably comments about the situation that will pertain after agreement, for example: "Then after we have (done this) we can ..." – "Once this stage is out of the way we will ..." If you watch any of the many property programmes on television, you will recognise how people move from making observations about a house to making comments about living in it. Such comments may well be interspersed with questions and other signs that some portion of the decision is still to be made; finally, the questions may only be for reassurance; in the person's own mind they have made the decision – and closing merely confirms and brings it out in the open.

You will come to trust your judgment in this area and it is well worth making a mental note of what signals you feel you see, and whether they provide an accurate indication of how things went on from there on, as a guide for the future.

## A first move

Closing is not a one-shot situation, some encounters involve a number of closes: with, for instance, the first rejected but the last agreed. One method of closing that may be used specifically to obtain feedback early on in a conversation – often with no real hope of actually closing at the point it is used – is the so-called "trial close". This can really be any kind of close in terms of technique: you may be pretty sure the answer will be a no, but the way what you say is phrased can be designed to give valuable clues as to how near you are getting to acceptance or on what element you should now concentrate to complete the process.

For example, if you attempt to close, the response might be someone saying something like: "Now wait a minute, we still need to discuss X", and you know to move on to discuss just that. This is a useful technique and can provide an alternative way of obtaining very focussed feedback at that crucial point in the conversation.

## Prompting final agreement

Closing, as has been said, is less a stage, rather it is often a simple question or comment. All you need is a particular choice of phraseology to match an individual and the circumstances. There are many permutations, but the most often used are perhaps the following (shown here linked to our running example about joining a committee):

- **Direct request:** Just a straight question: for example, "Shall we go ahead and put you on it then?" Requests like this should be used where the person likes to make their own decisions.
- **Command:** This effectively says: "Do this", perhaps linking it to what logically follows: "With that done you can ..." So, here: "Put the next meeting date in your diary and we'll include you from then on." This is effectively an instruction, so must be used with some care. This can be used where someone has difficulty in making a decision or has considerable respect for you.

- **Immediate gain:** For example, "You said you were free on 27th, so if you can give me the go-ahead about joining today, I can make sure that you get all the necessary papers well ahead of your first meeting." This could be used where, by acting fast, someone can get a particular benefit, whereas delay might cause certain or severe problems. Here, deciding today makes it easy to attend the next committee meeting date. The "hard" version of this is the so-called fear close, next.

- **Fear close:** As in something like: "Unless you decide today, you will miss the next meeting date", followed by stating the penalties of delay. This is a more powerfully phrased version of "immediate gain", and should perhaps be used with some discretion.

- **Alternatives:** effectively the "yes or yes approach". For example, "Do you want to attend on Tuesday next week, or would next month's meeting suit better?" A yes to either gives you agreement. If necessary, you can go on to pose other alternatives should a first one not achieve what you want. So, in this case perhaps: "Would you like simply to join or come along informally to one meeting to check us out?" (Incidentally, this technique always reminds me of the reply I received when conducting a sales workshop for the sales team at a large hotel when I asked a delegate to give me an example of an alternative close. They said, "That's when you say, 'Are you going to book here or at the Holiday Inn?'" Not the right answer! But I digress again). This method could be used where you are happy to get a commitment on any one of the possible alternatives.

- **"Best solution":** combines a question with recapping key issues, usually benefits. For example, "Once you are a member of the committee, you will find it's interesting and worthwhile, and that the time commitment really is manageable. Can you attend a first meeting on Tuesday week?" To be used when there is any complexity or when a number of different issues are in play; it is also appropriate when the other person is considering more than one way forward.

- **Question or objection:** For example, "If I can persuade you that the time commitment can be kept under control, would you give it a go?" To be used where you know you can answer the objection satisfactorily.

- **Assumption:** For example, "Fine. I've got all the information I need to get you on the committee. Once I get back to my desk I'll send you the minutes of the last meeting, and agenda for the next and all you have to do is be there on the day." Effectively you assume the person has said yes and continue the conversation on this basis.
- **Concession:** Here you trade only a small concession to get agreement now or agree to proceed only on stage one. For example, "If you agree to join I will guarantee that you do not collect any chores that involve writing; I know you spend so much time doing that already. How about it?"

Going back again to the presentation example, a final phrase to organise the presentation rehearsal might include such as:

- Just asking ("Shall we put a time in our diary?").
- Telling them – you may not have the authority to instruct them, but make it sound like an order – ("Put something in your diary").
- Suggesting why it is a good idea to commit now rather than later ("Let's set a date now, while we can find a mutually convenient time that does not disrupt anything else too much.").
- Or suggest why it is a bad idea to leave it ("Unless we set a date now, we will never find a convenient time before the presentation date.").
- Laying out alternatives, positive alternatives where agreement to either one gives you your own way ("So, shall we clear an hour for this or make it two?). And repeating as necessary ("So, an hour it is then, this week or next?).
- Assuming agreement and phrasing the request accordingly ("Fine, we seem to be agreed, let's get our diaries out and schedule a time.").

However you decide to phrase things – and in every case it should be firmly done and well timed – and whatever kind of close you select and use, the key thing here is to take the initiative and actually initiate a conclusion. You need to do so firmly, do so more than once if necessary and do so with everyone at every stage of the process.

Finally, to end this chapter let me quote American business guru Tom Hopkins: "It's the winning score, the bottom line, the name of the game, the cutting edge, the point of it all …unless you can close, you're like a football team that can't sustain a drive long enough to score. It's no good if you play your whole game in your own territory and never get across the goal line. So welcome to the delightful world of closing. If you don't love it now, start falling in love, because that's where the money is."

He was laying it on a bit thick because it is so important.

But a focus on getting whatever agreement you are after must pervade everything you do and, not least, it must ensure that you finish what you do in a way that gives you the best possible chance of success. Hopkins is not just talking about technique; he is also talking about motivation. Successful persuaders want to succeed, they aim to succeed (and believe they can) and are prepared to see the thing right through, despite the risk of a proportion of encounters ending in rejection. They know that failing to close too often means failing to get agreement.

---

**KEY DIFFERENTIATING FACTORS:**
Again this is easily stated: *always take the initiative and ask for agreement. Anything less can let agreement go by default.*

---

What next? At this stage, especially if you have been handling matters well, all may be concluded. "Yes", they say and agreement is made. This can happen, but sometimes (more often?) it will not: hence the next chapter.

# Chapter 7

# BEYOND THE CLOSE
## Follow through action

'Nothing in the world can take
the place of persistence.'
*Cavin Coolidge*

At the end of a conversation if agreement has been reached, then there may be no more to do, at least for the moment. But perhaps the conclusion is not the conclusion you want and, while someone is not saying, "No", they are not saying "Yes" either – so what do you do about the maybes?

---

**KEY DIFFERENTIATING FACTORS:**
Again let's put this up front: *without action to follow matters up and see them through to a (positive) conclusion, agreement may run into the sand.*

---

### AN ANTIDOTE TO "MAYBE"
People may say a number of things other than "Yes" or "No", and many people find the most difficult thing to deal with is that little phrase, "Let me think about it", which constitutes the ultimate "maybe".

### Dealing with "maybe"
A "maybe" response is essentially positive, yet if you just walk away

from it – helpfully allowing them to do just that – then you may never get another chance to move to agreement. Sometimes people who say this do actually mean, "No". They may feel that it is an easier and more polite route than just saying, "Get lost". But you need to know whether to take it at face value or not. So what is your best response?

It is often very difficult to think of a reason why someone should not think about it (unless perhaps you can contribute pressing reasons to decide at once). So the best route may well be to agree – and not simply to agree but to urge them to think about it. Tell them it is an important decision, tell them they must not make it lightly, tell them they should not be rushed, that they must be certain; however you phrase it, make sure you are clearly on the side of thinking about it. As their expectation of you is probably something more argumentative, this response is usually accepted and allows you to go further.

Then you can go on to ask why exactly they still need to think about it, or what elements of the decision they feel still need review. Often something is then volunteered at this point. There is a particular sticking point, something about the case has been less well made than the rest, or there is some area where more information seems to be needed. Then you can try turning the intention back to more discussion, as in this example about an undefined project:

*"Let me think about it".*
*"Of course, it's a big decision, you have to be sure".*
*"That's right".*
*"You must be sure it's right in every respect; is there any particular aspect which you need to think about particularly?"*
*"Well, I suppose it's the timescale that worries me most. It would be bound to affect current work".*
*"To some extent yes, but we can minimise that. Perhaps I didn't explain how we would approach that sufficiently clearly; can I go over it again before we finish?"*
*"Okay. I want to have it all straight in my mind".*

The conversation or meeting is thus set under way again and there is no reason why it cannot move on towards another close, which may then be agreed without any further wish to think about it being expressed.

This phrase is regularly a sign that something – and it may be several somethings, in which case you may be able to get the individual to list them before you suggest more discussion – is still unclear or unresolved.

But another situation may be in evidence. Someone may ask for time to think about it not because they need time to think, but for some other reason. Perhaps the two most likely are the need to confer with someone else (are they, in fact, the ultimate decision maker?), or maybe there is something with which they want to make a comparison and they need time to check out the alternative option. In this case, careful questioning may discover either possibility, or indeed others. Then the action on which you plan to close may change; maybe the first step is to try to organise a meeting with their colleague or whoever else is involved (sometimes they appreciate help with any persuasion that may be necessary, as, for example, when someone needs to involve say their partner or boss and wants to be sure they do approve).

Again we see that the better the quality of the information you find out at every stage, the better position you are in to take things further. Such techniques are not infallible, but if they increase your strike rate even a little they are well worth pursuing, and you may be surprised by how often, "Let me think about it" leads not to thinking about it, but to extended discussion and then a – positive – decision.

**After they say "Yes"**
Assuming you are going to achieve a good strike rate – think positive! – then some of the people you communicate with will agree. Then what? Well, the first thing is to thank them, you do not need to grovel, and you need to bear the nature of the relationship in mind, but a thank you costs nothing and may well be both highly appropriate and much appreciated. It is good practice to couple the thanks with reassurance: "Thanks very much, John; I am sure we will find this works out well all round." Then consider any practical points that need to be dealt with at this stage:

- Must documentation be completed (some kind of formal deal may involve confirmation, contracts and so on)?
- Do you need a signature?

- What further information do you need (an agreed date, a reference number, an e-mail address so that you can keep in touch)?
- Are there points still to be discussed/agreed (especially things running on into the future: once a first stage is passed, what then)?

Everything of this nature must be dealt with in a prompt and business-like way – you are still on show and it is still possible at this stage for someone to change their mind, demand to negotiate a different arrangement, or simply say, "I've been thinking and rescind the agreement" – something that would negate the result you think you have achieved. So deal with such things promptly and end the conversation.

Do not chatter on in a fit of euphoria; many a person has talked themselves out of an agreement again at this stage. Of course, some social chat may well be important and there are deals where both parties regard lunch afterwards as natural. But do be a little careful. Be sure that whomever you are dealing with – who no doubt values their time highly – really wants to extend the dialogue. And decide the objectives of such an extended meeting (especially if it is part of or the start of a working relationship).

In formal circumstances, do you drop business, talk no "shop" and treat it socially, or use it to move on to other topics? It is important to make the other person comfortable in this respect. They may not like it if they planned to use the time constructively and you just talk of golf; or vice versa. It is often useful to bear in mind that you have moved on and discourage revisiting the decision if you feel that might end in a revised view.

When you have gone your separate ways, never fail to double check that your paperwork or notes are completed. People have been known to forget something vital – a figure or other detail – particularly after a good lunch! There may be occasions where a written thank you might be appropriate too. This can be combined with the business element of an arrangement, for instance a new committee member might get a thank you with the agenda for the next meeting – the first they will attend. Some occasions may need more; even a gift.

When you have obtained agreement, then any persuasive communication may be at an end (though it may be the beginning of an ongoing dialogue to hold and develop the relationship with someone); but there is more to bear in mind when things are not clear and longer term contact is necessary.

## Persistence and long-term contact

You will know the old saying: 'out of sight, out of mind' and it is one worth bearing in mind if you seek to get an agreement which will, it is clear, take some time. The possible timescale varies a good deal and may sometimes be lengthy.

I once maintained contact with a client for almost three years during which I got no work from them at all. I met them once during this time, and we had maybe eight or nine other contacts, which took a variety of forms: I telephoned, wrote letters and e-mailed. Then I got a response – and the single largest piece of work I have booked at one go in twenty years. The time – very little – it took to stay in touch was vanishingly insignificant compared with the return. It is good, incidentally, to ring the changes on method in such circumstances, remembering that a telephone call leaves no permanent reminder, a written note can be filed or slipped in a diary, and that an e-mail, while being quick and easy to send, can be deleted in the blink of a mouse's eye.

Be persistent and be organised in your persistence; it's an important contributor to success. Do not let too long go by without a reminder, yet do not become a nuisance either; some careful judgement is necessary here depending on the circumstances and who it is that you are chasing. Because it can be awkward, embarrassing even, to maintain contact like this – "Whatever do I say next?" – the rule should be not to put it off but to be disciplined about planning and making the next contact. What influences that contact and when it is done should be your view of the other person and what is necessary and appropriate for them, rather than simply when it is convenient for you.

If you work with someone or see them regularly, this may be simple. But with someone you know less well it may be more difficult, especially if you are getting signals that, rightly or wrongly, put you off going further: you telephone and get no reply or are told they're in a meeting, they're away or just they're busy. So, apart from gritting your teeth and making yourself make one more phone call or whatever, you may occasionally need to think of something a bit more memorable to do to try and prod someone into action.

An example comes from my own writing work. Following writing a short book for another specialist publisher, I was keen to undertake a topic for them in the same format. I proposed the idea and got a generally good reaction to my suggested topic – but no confirmation. I wrote and telephoned a number of times. Weeks turned to months as my reminders continued – but no reply came. Always I received a delay or a put off (you may know the feeling!). Finally, when a reminder of the possibility came up yet again from my follow-up system, I felt I had exhausted all the conventional possibilities, so I sat down, wrote the following and printed it out on my letterhead.

*Struggling author: patient, reliable (non-smoker), seeks commission on business topics. Novel formats preferred, but anything considered within reason. Ideally a text of 100 or so pages, on a topic like sales excellence sounds good; maybe with some illustrations. Delivery of the right quantity of material – on time – guaranteed. Contact me at the above address/telephone number or let's meet on neutral ground, carrying a copy of* Publishing News *and wearing a carnation.*

After hesitating a little over whether to send it (it was to go to someone I had only met once), at the end of the day I decided it was not too much over the top and I signed and posted it. Gratifyingly an e-mail confirmation came by the middle of the morning on the following day, and said they liked what I had sent – irresistible. (Incidentally, you can now read the result – *The Sales Excellence Pocketbook,* Management Pocketbooks.) As so often here, the proposition had been well received, but circumstances then conspired to delay a response. After all, it is often more important to us to get an agreement than it is for the other person to make it. People are busy and what we regard as a priority may simply go on their back burner; such things then need a nudge and something a little out of the ordinary may well do the trick.

So, don't reject anything other than the conventional approach; try a little experiment and see what it can do for you. But, above all, having put over a good case, do not let your good work wither on the vine – keep in touch and you make ultimately gaining a commitment more likely.

As a final and perhaps unconventional approach, let me end this chapter by suggesting there are occasions when not being persuasive can be the most persuasive thing to do!

## Success through non-persuasion

Modesty is said to be the art of encouraging people to find out for themselves just how wonderful you are; in the same way not being "persuasive" can sometimes persuade people to go along with you. Certainly in a sales situation, a customer may want and need to do business with and through a sales person, but they may also want expert support and advice from someone that they feel they can trust. Too often they actually believe that this is the last thing they will get, that the sales person is only out for themselves and that if they shake hands with them they should count their fingers afterwards to check they are still all present. Sometimes, however, they find that they feel they really can trust a sales person, and this is true of any persuasive situation.

Various things can be used to help people come more certainly to that conclusion: not being too "pushy" and exerting undue pressure, for instance. Another method can be introduced with more positive intent: literally saying that you are not trying to persuade. How do you do this? With phrases such as: "I believe honesty is always best, so let me tell you ..." "If I were trying to twist your arm, I probably wouldn't tell you this, but let me say ...." Effectively, you let them see what you might do, making the point that doing so would make, and then avoid doing it. In a way it doubles the power.

In competitive situations, you can even get people focusing more on the techniques of another person trying to persuade them towards some other decision than on what they say, by referring to their techniques specifically: "Now I know John has a clever answer to the objection you raise, but let me be honest, I know it is a problem, but it can be overcome by ..." Next time they see your rival they may well notice what they say on the topic and be inclined to be more suspicious of it than would otherwise have been the case.

Do not overuse such an approach and always be carefully or it can easily sound glib. But a regular tone of this sort within your conversation can add the feeling to the conviction that you really do put the other person's needs ahead of pushing them into whatever action you want of them. Take care with this approach, but remember there are many people that will take some display of modesty as a sign that there is strength, expertise and other good qualities underneath – and who will dismiss any overt brashness as not to be trusted.

And finally, although being persistent can put you in embarrassing situations, this is only a psychological problem. The logic for being persistent is inescapable, and it can quickly pay dividends in terms of strike rate.

# Afterword

# Action for the future

'Everyone lives by selling something.'
*Robert Louis Stevenson*

Communication is a permanent underlying thread to most peoples' work. Most of the time we may think little about it. But we do notice quickly enough when something goes wrong. Never forget that communication can be inherently difficult. It works more effectively and more certainly when it is thought about, when the message is well considered. This is doubly so if there are any special factors involved, and communicating persuasively – setting out to get your own way – is certainly a greater challenge than simpler forms of communication.

If I have done my job then from the earlier chapters you will have got a flavour of how to be persuasive, and how to present a compelling case – one that will give someone reasons to agree. There may be no simple magic formula that guarantees success, but, as we have seen, there are a number of principles and techniques that smooth the way and make getting agreement more likely. While you will never win them all, as it were, you should certainly be able to achieve a good strike rate.

One thing's for sure: persuasion cannot be deployed "by rote". There can be no "script", and although there are guiding principles, there is no single set way of proceeding that allows you simply to follow the rules on "automatic pilot", as it were, each time. Always remember that the approach you take needs to be decided, case by case, person by person.

Similar thinking may be involved in analysing a situation and deciding on the precise approach you will adopt, but what works today with one person is just that. Tomorrow, next week, next year, or with someone else, something different may be needed. And the adaptation might involve changing a word or two, or adopting a radically different approach.

Persuasive communication must be approached in an individual way, and as circumstances change – who you are aiming to persuade, how they think and what affects them and so on – the approach needs to accommodate them. Thus we will all spend a lifetime honing our persuasive communication skills, not only to become better at deploying them, but also to better fit them to whatever the current circumstances may demand. Recognising that this is necessary is the first step towards keeping your skills ahead of the game and maintaining an acceptable success rate.

Practice makes perfect. You need to bear in mind the guidelines set out here and give them a try. If things do not go perfectly at first, no matter, but everything you do should be a step in the right direction. The trick is to learn from your experience, to observe and recognise what went well and what went less well, and adapt your approach as time goes by. Some sports person (it's usually quoted as a golfer) once said, "It's a funny thing, but the more I practice, the more my luck seems to improve." There is surely a clear truth expressed here – one with a moral.

### Maximising the chances of success

A wealth of detail is involved here; witness the rest of this text, but let's conclude with just three points that, while not negating any others, are especially important. You should:

- **Prepare carefully:** so much stems from the thought you put in before you even open your mouth. Preparation is key. Make time to do it, make it constructive and everything that follows will be that little bit easier.
- **Adopt a consciousness of the whole process:** being aware of the processes, approaches and techniques and how they all fit together is the first step to deploying them in a way that makes for

effectiveness. The orchestration of all this may seem difficult at first, but the habit of keeping the overview in mind builds up, especially if you aim that it should, and this quickly begins to make the process easier and more manageable.

- **Focus on the other person:** being persuasive is not, remember, something you do to people. This is sufficiently important to be worth quoting a memorable example, which I should perhaps mention is from my book *100 Great Sales Ideas*, Marshall Cavendish.

  The television series *Star Trek* is now a legend across the globe. The original series may have started slowly, but it gained cult status, spawned several spin-off series across many years and led to an ongoing series of successful movies. Financially, it is one of the most successful such franchises ever. Yet it may be difficult now to remember how different it was at its inception from other programmes broadcast at the time. Gene Roddenberry had to find a way of pitching his novel programme idea to the networks. He knew that those he sought to persuade were conservative and that many programmes accepted were actually close to something already existing. The classic "known quantity" seemed to be important and *Star Trek* initially proved very difficult to sell as he enthused about its uniqueness. One of the most successful series at the time was the western series – Wagon Train. But the circumstances of the characters, a tight knit group, moving on to pastures new, each episode showing what happens to them in the new location and with the people they meet there, were essentially similar to his space odyssey idea. He finally sold *Star Trek* by describing it, in four powerful words, as "Wagon Train in space". This was then a well-chosen analogy and people understood and, despite the risk of something so new and different, he got agreement to make the programme. The rest, as they say, is history. The thinking this illustrates, that of describing something in terms that the other person will relate to, is clear – and a useful thought to bear in mind for any of us trying to be persuasive

- **Be confident:** if you have thought through what you intend to do, if it is based on sound principles and you know that this is the case, then you can afford to be confident. There is a virtuous circle here. Being confident shows. The case you make is then judged differently. It may seem more credible if you have the courage of your convictions and, if so, then as it begins to work, positive feedback can raise your confidence still more.

Recognise that all this is possible: if you see the necessity for a considered approach and go about building your case with care and putting it over with precision, then you may well surprise yourself with just how persuasive you can be.

What is needed for the future is that you:

- Link in the techniques reviewed to the other stock in trade expertise that you use in your work so that they enhance your overall approach to communicating.
- Deploy the techniques in such a way that, while they contribute to your persuasiveness, people continue to see you in a positive light: as reasonable, approachable, and/or whatever else is relevant.
- Deploy them on a "bespoke" basis, so that what is done is always tailored person by person and meeting by meeting to the individual circumstances and the person (or people) you want to persuade. It is too simplistic to think that there are a few, standard persuasive approaches that can be deployed every time in exactly the same way.

Many people initially baulk at the thought of being persuasive – "I can't be pushy" – though, in my experience, once they set their mind to it (and what you have to do may demand it), find that persuasive communication techniques can go comfortably alongside their normal reasonable persona. They find that their profile is enhanced, not least by the confidence that knowing what they are doing allows them to project, and that so too are the results that they achieve in securing agreement and effectively getting their own way.

It is always satisfying when you succeed at something like this. Sometimes what is wanted is achieved easily, but more often circumstances need the right approach to be carefully deployed if agreement is to be forthcoming. It is then even more satisfying when you succeed and you can look back, sometimes at a long complex chain of events, and say, "I made that happen".

You now know something of the techniques that will allow you to do just that. I have made it clear that luck is not the most important thing here, so I will not end by wishing you good luck, but I wish you well with it.

# Patrick Forsyth

Patrick Forsyth began his career in publishing and has run Touchstone Training & Consultancy since 1990; this specialises in the improvement of marketing, management and communications skills. He is an experienced conference speaker and writes extensively on business matters. He is the author of many successful books on aspects of business, management and careers, including *How to Write Reports and*  *Proposals* (Kogan Page) and *Marketing: A Guide to the Fundamentals* (The Economist).

One reviewer says of his work: "Patrick has a lucid and elegant style of writing which allows him to present information in a way that is organised, focussed and easy to apply."

## Other Books in Smart Skills Series

Meetings

Working with Others

Negotiation

Presentations

Mastering the Numbers

www.smartskillsbooks.com

www.legendpress.co.uk

www.twitter.com/legend_press